Ten Tales of Two Wheeled Touring

Ian Cameron

3rd edition March 2021

By the same author:
More Tales of Two Wheeled Touring (2021)
Fun on the Run (2021)

Contents

Why this book?

The tours:

3

This book is dedicated to both my wife, Chris, who has unwaveringly encouraged me to participate in my passion for cycle touring, but also to all of my cycling buddies whose company I have shared on many trips and who suggested that I recount our adventures by writing this book

Why this book?

Quite simply, to amuse and inform those who like reading about cycling tours, and to encourage non-cyclists to try out a cycling holiday.

I was once a non-cyclist too – here's how I started:

Some may remember the 1990's "**Health at Work**" initiative aimed at promoting healthy NHS staff as role models in an effort to encourage the general public to follow suit.

With some responsibility for delivering "Health at Work" locally, I decided I should be seen to be leading from the front, so I undertook to join the programme's first cycling event – a 50 mile bike ride from **Liverpool to Chester** and back.

But I did not own a bike!

I purchased an Apollo mountain bike from Halfords for £99.00. It was steel framed and had fat, nobbly, tyres. It was really unsuitable for road riding, but hey, I felt so proud, as I'd never owned a shiny, brand-new, bike before.

On the day of the ride I was accompanied by a colleague who didn't possess a bike either. He'd borrowed his wife's step-through, three geared, Raleigh. We safely made it through the Mersey Tunnel and cycled through Wirral villages to the halfway point at the Countess of Chester Hospital where I rubbed shoulders with Chris Boardman - the event's inspirational celebrity. After a sandwich lunch, it was time to ride back again.

Despite my inappropriate bike, I was smitten by the atmosphere of riding with 300 others and I suddenly felt like I was a cyclist!

A couple of years after my debut, I spotted an advert for a week-long "Cycling Safari" in Ireland. It sounded like an interesting and unusual holiday, so my wife and I signed up. Bikes were supplied and luggage transported to our accommodation. The 35-miles-a-day route started in Cork and after following a rural route across to Bantry Bay in the west, returned to Cork along the south coast. The group was an entertaining mix of 15 people and I was sold on the concept of cycle touring.

In 2002, a work colleague asked if I'd be interested in joining a small group planning to cycle the 130-mile Coast to Coast cycle route between Workington and Sunderland. That sounded like even more fun, so I purchased a pair of £19.99 pannier bags from Argos and thus began nearly two decades of regular cycle touring.

During all of my tours, which number around 30, I have had hugely enjoyable experiences peppered with amusing incidents. It would take several books to describe them all so I have selected ten of the best to share. They cover tours in England, Scotland and Wales plus two of the "must do" cycling challenges – London to Paris, and Land's End to John O'Groats.

All of these tours took place between 2002 and 2019. My touring plans for 2020 were scuppered due to the Covid19 pandemic so instead, I used the time to revisit my personal tour logs and write this book.

I do hope my tales of touring on two wheels will inspire others to participate in active holidays, or at least for cyclists and non-cyclists alike to simply sit back and enjoy the tour descriptions.

1. Sea to Sea – Workington to Sunderland

Background

The invitation from my work colleague was too tempting to resist. We had become aware of the 130 mile C2C (Coast to Coast) route as a classic cycle challenge on a par with the famous Coast to Coast walk.

As beginners, we were relieved to find that the route was signposted and a Sustrans map was available. What could possibly go wrong?

Of the seven who signed up for the trip, I was the one with the most available time so it fell to me to do some research and work out a few logistics. In hindsight, starting preparations in late-May, for a tour five weeks later, was not the best idea.

Travel logistics

How do you transport seven people, seven bikes and associated pannier bags from home to Workington and then back again from Sunderland?

We wanted to start early on a Friday morning and be back again the following Sunday evening to avoid using precious holiday entitlement. Train travel was too inflexible. This left car travel as the obvious choice, especially after I located Ted Gillman of Tyne Valley Holidays who was willing to collect two cars from Workington and have them ready for us in Sunderland two days later.

I'd also found the name of a chap in Workington who had a secure compound for our cars while they awaited collection.

Sue's car comfortably accommodated four passengers, with three bikes on a towbar-mounted bike rack. My Nissan

Primera, was able to squash three of us, our bags, and two bikes, all inside the car. The other two bikes swayed around alarmingly on a borrowed boot-mounted bike rack.

Accommodation

Due to our late preparations, finding vacant accommodation for seven people in both Penrith and Alston was tricky. Luckily, one fully booked proprietor in Penrith recommended her friend at another guest house. She was just staring out and had vacancies. Everywhere in Alston was fully booked, but the Packhorse Inn in nearby Stanhope could accommodate us. Hurrah!

Bikes and kit

Ged, an experienced and regular road cyclist had a good touring bike. Mark and Sue had toured previously in Cornwall and possessed a pair of half decent hybrids, but after that we had a right jumble of less-than-suitable equipment. Seta was riding a borrowed mountain bike, a size too small and her husband, Peter, had a hybrid which looked like he'd just got it out of the shed that morning. Nat's bike was adequate but we were not sure if she'd done any training. I definitely had done no training but had purchased a brand new Raleigh P100 mountain bike in Halford's sale. It was also a size too small for me but at £200, reduced to £133, it seemed a bargain.

As most of us knew each other through a running club our clothing tended to be unsuitable short sleeved tee shirts and lightweight running jackets.

Friday: Travel to the start

I was pleased that I had packed the bikes the night before. After a quick wash, I dressed and threw a cup of tea down before picking up Ged at 05.45 then Nat at 06.00. The plan was to drive up the M6 and meet the others in Workington at around nine o'clock.

I was once travelling northwards on the M6 when the traffic unexpectedly started braking and swerving to avoid what turned out to be a girl's bike lying in the centre lane. A quarter of a mile further on, a family of four stood next to a stationary car sporting a now empty bike rack. They were all gazing back down the carriageway.

I did not fancy a similar experience, and with two bikes rattling around on my rack, I kept my speed down. At Penrith we turned on to the A66 through Keswick to Cockermouth. By now, I was craving my fix of morning caffeine so pulled in at a high street cafe. It was nine-fifteen and the cafe had just opened. We piled in and phoned the others.

"How will we know which cafe you're in?" they asked.

"Err, 'cos ours is the only car in the High Street with two bikes on the back!"

The cafe staff were at sixes and sevens sorting themselves out but eventually we were served with coffee and bagels. We probably left at 10.15. Time was ticking on.

We travelled in convoy to Workington where we located the chap with the secure compound. It seemed odd and a bit risky handing over bunches of car keys to a complete stranger.

There followed much faffing around as pannier bags were fitted on bikes and tyres inflated. Not having ridden with pannier bags before, I couldn't understand why my heels kept catching until Mark pointed out that I'd mounted them the wrong way round. Doh!

Then everyone wanted the loo before we finally set off.

I'd read somewhere that it was customary on the C2C to dip your wheels into the Irish Sea at the start and into the North Sea at the finish. Luckily "compound man" agreed to show us to the beach and take the photograph.

It was probably 11.40 before we finally started, a bit late in the day, to commence a 48 mile ride.

The ride

The initial route was promising enough as we rode along the course of an old railway line, but soon after starting, we all stopped while Sue took a long phone call from her boss who didn't realise she wasn't in work.

After cycling ten miles, we found ourselves back in Cockermouth. It was 12.45 and as far as I was concerned, that meant lunchtime. But with 38 miles still to go, my suggestion was laughed out of court and we pressed on.

With sat nav not available for another 12 years, we were reliant on following the blue, National Cycle Network signs. Whilst they were generally easy to spot, we found that about 5% were missing, facing in confusing directions or obscured by foliage. Progress was slow.

Just before Bassenthwaite Lake, we opted for an off road section through

Wythop Woods. This pretty trail climbed up before dropping steeply down towards the lake. I'd failed to check my new bike properly and whilst hard braking during a steep descent, my brake cables slipped leaving me with no means of stopping and an ever accelerating speed. To avoid a serious crash I had to lean to the side, put my foot hard down to the ground and slide my body off to the side. Mark quickly identified the problem and after tightening the screws on the brake callipers I resumed the ride, ashen faced.

By the time we reached Keswick, it was raining hard. Nat's bare hands were freezing so we stopped while she purchased some gloves. The C2C route continued to the town's swimming pool where we used its canopy to shelter whilst eating our lunchtime sandwiches. It was 2.30 and we'd completed 26 miles.

The old railway line through Threlkeld provided a good traffic-free stretch but while negotiating a short, narrow, section, Mark succeeded in shoulder charging me into a ditch, luckily with a soft landing.

We continued to follow the blue signs, including an unnecessary 4 mile loop via Mungrisdale and back to the A66. Shortly, the official route again looped north but being totally soaked and fatigued, the vote was to continue riding at the side of the A66 directly to Penrith.

I'm guessing it was around 5.30 when we reached the town centre and the Guest House. After we rang the bell, a formidable landlady opened her front door and shouted, "STOP!" before directing us round the block to the back door. Here she ordered us to take off our wet shoes and place them on the newspaper she'd carefully laid out. Wet coats went into an outbuilding before we were finally allowed in.

19

We'd not arranged anywhere for an evening meal so after sorting myself out, I walked up the main street looking for suitable eateries. In terms of dining out, Penrith is not Padstow, but I did find a decent looking Italian restaurant and booked us in for 8pm.

When we arrived, they weren't quite ready for us so we repaired to a local bar and sank a pint of lager, or three.

Back at the guest house, I fell asleep as soon as my head touched the pillow.

Saturday

What a change in the weather with the sun out, making for a happy atmosphere within the group. Despite consuming our Italian meal less than twelve hours previously, we managed to give a good account of ourselves at the breakfast table. We didn't know it at the time, but we would need that fuel for what lay ahead.

With fewer junctions, the blue signs seemed easier to follow as we climbed higher and higher. We'd heard about the brutal climb to the highest point at Hartside Summit but we simply put our bikes into our lowest gears and kept turning the pedals grinding out the miles. Eventually we reached the cafe at 16 miles, so ideal for a coffee stop. The views were magnificent.

The day continued with descents and climbs and more descents and more climbs, through gorgeous scenery until we reached the village of Nenthead. Here, a carnival was in full swing with the main street closed and a live band playing. It was a great place to stop to rehydrate and it was so tempting to tarry but we had more miles to ride so we forced ourselves back in the saddle.

Eventually we rolled into Stanhope, whose main features seemed to be a petrified tree stump in the churchyard and 50's TV presenter, Muriel Young's birthplace. We easily found our accommodation at the Packhorse Inn, on the main street, and our bikes were securely stored in the beer cellar. We pre-ordered our evening meal and inspected our rooms. Just the doubles seemed to be en suite so for Nat, Ged and I it was a case of listening at the bathroom door to see if it was free.

So what does one do in Stanhope on a Saturday night? The only action seemed to be a karaoke night at the rival Bonny Moorhen pub opposite. I can't say it was packed - probably about 15 people at most. I'd never done karaoke before but after a few beers, what the heck. I felt my "Mack the Knife" was passable as was "Don't get around much anymore", but clearly the punters wanted something more modern. The three girls did "Mustang Sally" but when I had a go at, "Do Wah Diddy Diddy", I noticed a definite thinning out of the clientele.

Sue's suggestion of a group rendition of that Beach Boys classic, "Good Vibrations", seemed a good idea until we attempted to sing what is, after all, a complicated arrangement with 4-part harmonies. This was the last straw - by the time we reached the end of the song, the bar was empty.

Sunday

At 37 miles, this was to be our shortest day. Well, it would have been had we not made a navigational error. We'd gone perhaps four miles before realising the mistake and had to ride four miles back into Stanhope. But that warm up may have been a blessing as the C2C signs pointed us up an almost vertical climb called "Crawleyside Bank". It was definitely a crawl. It was so slow that on a sharp bend with a steep camber, Ged, our most experienced rider, lost his momentum, overbalanced and toppled off.

Once we'd conquered this very long climb we felt on top of the world in glorious and remote moorland. It was well worth the effort.

After a further 14 miles, the scenery changed as we drifted into Consett, once a prosperous industrial area but now a sad reflection of its former self.

Broken glass occasionally spattered the trail as we commenced our long descent to the coast. Ged suffered the only puncture of the day but wearing surgeon-type rubber gloves completed the operation quickly and expertly.

The run into Sunderland along the River Wear was a delight and at the appointed time of 5pm, we reached the harbour and spotted our cars, with Ted sunbathing alongside. We paid a quick visit to Roker Beach for the obligatory "Wheels in the North Sea" photograph before grabbing a hot shower in the sailing club.

By the time we'd loaded the bikes it was 6pm as we began our trek home. To be honest, a 190 mile drive was not what I wanted at the end of a tough tour. My two passengers quickly fell asleep but I drove on. At Hartshead Services on the M62 near Bradford, I definitely needed a break and some caffeine.

We finally rolled into Wirral at about 11.30. I dropped off my compadres, plus their bikes, before returning home and crashing into my bed at half past midnight.

Summary
What a great introduction to self-planned cycle touring with superb scenery and reasonable daily mileages (48, 45 and 37). Huge fun and a big sense of achievement – I even had some commemorative sports shields made for the participants. And we definitely had bragging rights at work the next day.

Learning points

This first self-organised tour was a learning experience for me. I undertook to do a few things differently on future tours including:

- Start planning early
- Examine routes and choose comfortable daily cycling distances
- Carefully plot the route with notes (this was pre-Garmin)
- Identify suitable stopping places with available overnight accommodation and meal opportunities
- Consider the travel options to the start and from the finish
- Prepare bikes carefully

2. The Way of the Roses – Morecambe to Bridlington

Background

My experiences of cycling the C2C route provided an unfulfilled appetite for another helping of coast to coast.

Planning-wise, The Way of the Roses route appeared to provide a readymade, 170 mile, trip which everyone would be able to navigate using the National Cycle Network direction signs.

After spreading the word, I ended up with a party of 16 riders.

My riding buddy, Roy, was not keen on taking his bike on a train, preferring instead to start tours from home in Wirral. I had a look at the logistics and his suggestion to ride to the start in Morecambe was indeed achievable.

Day 1: Friday
After early starts, three of us rode to the Mersey ferry terminal and boarded the first sailing of the day. It was a very cold April morning but the weather forecast promised a warmer day later.

From Liverpool Pier Head we progressed out of the city on the quiet Dock Road before joining a traffic-free trail and rural lanes to the Lancashire market town of Ormskirk.

Here, we met more of our party who had used the local train service thus removing about 20 miles from their day's cycle. Our rendezvous was at Costa Coffee where we knew we were guaranteed lattes and artisan toast.

From Ormskirk, we rode along more picturesque Lancashire lanes. At Clayton-le-Woods we picked up the Lancashire Cycleway through the serene Cuerdon Valley Park before crossing the River Ribble at Penworthan Bridge. Here we joined the Preston Guild cycleway to our lunch stop at the excellent Brockholes Nature Reserve.

Brockholes is a former gravel quarry transformed by The RSPB and The Lancashire Wildlife Trust into a 250 acre sanctuary with habitats to encourage different species of wildlife to visit across the whole year. The centre also boasts a superb cafe with log burning stove and extensive meal choices. It's one of those stops where you just want to stay all day.

But we needed to burn some miles, so we continued along the Preston Guild cycle route before taking a series of unclassified roads north. We criss-crossed the M6 a few times before reaching the Canalside Cafe at Galgate - another excellent refreshment stop.

Our final leg took us on the Lancashire Coastal Way – a cycle route alongside the atmospheric River Lune all the way into Lancaster. Here we joined a former railway line (now a dedicated cycle path) into Morecambe.

Those who had been working during the day caught evening trains and all sixteen of us gathered for a meal at a local restaurant. Jill used the opportunity to tidy up her bum bag, discarding any waste and tearing up her train tickets.

Day 2: Saturday

We met by the Eric Morecambe statue for a group photograph before making our way to the official Way of the Roses start near to the impressive art deco Midland Hotel on the seafront.

At 09.30, we commenced our 49 mile ride to Grassington. Whilst 49 miles may seem a little light, we knew we were in for some serious climbing. The lanes were quiet and the scenery spectacular as we climbed out of Lancaster and on to High Bentham and on again to Settle.

Here, I popped into the Three Peaks bike shop to ask them to examine a worrying clunking noise coming from my bike's bottom bracket. It was no problem for them to take a quick look and to lubricate a dry component. I paid just £5.00 but as I was leaving, the mechanic asked if I was doing The Way of the Roses route. When I said, "Yes", he warned me about attempting to cycle up the climb out of Settle. "You could end up breaking your chain, mate", he advised.

I soon reached the climb he'd referred to. Crikey! I couldn't have cycled up that brute if I'd had no pannier bags and an electric motor. All of our party were similarly beaten and had to dismount except for our two wiry and highly competitive riders, Mark and Pete, who made it to the top.

The route over the moors continued to enthral the team. A good tail wind soon powered us on to the quaint village of Grassington, our overnight stop. Shortages of suitable accommodation had resulted in the group being billeted across a number of hotels and B&Bs nearby.

I was in a sub-group of four who were booked into a holiday park located two and a half miles outside the village. Not only had we secured four single rooms in the main house but had bragged to the others about our on-site swimming pool and sauna.

We'd arrived a little later than planned but we agreed between us that after sorting our bags out and ringing home, we'd fit in a quick swim before heading off to explore the fleshpots of Grassington. Shortly, Roy knocked on my door to suggest that a swim would encroach on valuable drinking time and that we should instead proceed directly to the pub in Grassington. Ceri agreed.

We banged on Fred's door to tell him about the revised arrangements but there was no answer. Had he fallen into a deep slumber we wondered? Fred was 81 and it had been a tough day for him. So, if he wasn't asleep, then what?

We began to think the unthinkable. We hammered even harder but still no reply.

In the end, I went to look for a member of staff who could open his door and make sure he was still breathing. The sign on the empty reception desk directed me to the leisure complex. I described the crisis.

"Have a look in the changing room", suggested the pool manager. Phew, there was Fred in all his glory, just about to step into his blue speedos.

We asked the receptionist about hiring a taxi to take the four of us into Grassington. We were dismayed to find that the nearest was in Skipton, about 10 miles away and that there would be a premium to cover the extra distance. We started walking but with a 7pm meal booked it became apparent that we needed an alternative strategy.

Yes, it was cheeky but we flagged down a couple of cars leaving the holiday park and blagged lifts into the village, arriving in time for a couple of scoops of Black Sheep Ale before our meal in The Foresters Arms.

Funny, but Ceri found a Grassington taxi firm's card in a phone box, so no problem returning to our digs.

Day 3: Sunday

We all assembled in Grassington's quaintly cobbled square ready to leave at 9.30.

Grassington

Well, not quite "all". Roy went to purchase some Spar sandwiches but on reaching the till realised he'd left his wallet back at the holiday park.

He told us not to wait but his detour put another five miles on to the 61 he was due to cycle that day.

Leaving Grassington, we continued on remote and stunning moorland roads. A long and gradual descent had the four girls singing along to a small, rack mounted, sound system. Soon, the following steep descent down to Pateley Bridge not only had many serious roadside warning signs but also worrying breaks in the safety barrier where those warnings had been ignored. We all had extremely hot brakes at the foot of the descent where we crossed the River Nidd.

After an initial climb back out of the valley, the road levelled off. The route took us through the gorgeous Studley Deer Park and water gardens before passing Fountains Abbey. This was another superb feature of this route. We arrived in the quaint market town of Ripon where we had lunch in one of the cafes in the square.

From Ripon, the route was more or less flat all the way into York, in contrast to what had gone before and a welcome change for the final miles of this 61 mile leg. We stayed overnight in a Premier Inn.

That evening our cycling group enjoyed an excellent Indian meal. The restaurant was opposite Whip Ma Whop Ma Gate (the shortest street in York, apparently).

Day 4: Monday

We assembled for a team photograph outside the main entrance to York Minster:

Our final 60 miles to Bridlington was less rugged so afforded faster cycling along flat lanes. After a coffee stop in Pocklington we continued to Driffield for lunch. Here, Adam found a Garden Centre serving roast dinners at a bargain price. Several foolishly participated. That's all very well until you try remounting and cycling a further 19 miles against the clock. There followed an unseemly and somewhat vulgar few miles of chronic belching.

I had not realised the size of Bridlington. After hitting the outskirts, we rode for perhaps another 4 miles before reaching the Way of the Roses finishing post on the promenade. It was 4pm so time for a quick team photograph before cycling just a mile and a half to Bridlington Station.

I had arranged for Bill to meet us in a hired van. This was to allow the group to travel home by train without having to reserve rare bikes spaces. The van hire plus £50.00 for Bill worked out at just £10.00 per person. Adam had arranged to travel back with Bill to keep him company.

As we were in a seaside town, we could not resist purchasing fish and chips before waiting for the train to Liverpool.

At this point Jill retrieved her train tickets only to discover that the tickets she'd ripped up back in Morecambe were the Bridlington to Liverpool tickets for herself and her husband, Pete. In her hand was a pair of useless three-day-old tickets between Liverpool and Morecambe.

Jill approached the official in the ticket office to explain what had happened, even showing him the email purchase confirmation but he was having none of it – purchase new (full price) tickets or don't travel.

Adam came up with a solution. Jill could travel in the van's cab and Pete could sit in the rear with the bikes. That was all very well but as I was the named hirer of the van, I was responsible for the terms and conditions to be honoured and I'm pretty sure it did not include the carriage of passengers in the load space. I found this out once I was on the train but had I known about the plan, well, I suspect I may have said yes anyway.

Apparently a few miles after leaving Bridlington, the trio in the cab heard loud banging. On investigation, they found it was Pete who could stand the noise and discomfort no longer. Adam invited him into the cab despite there being only three seats and three seat belts. It is a wonder they were not pulled over by police but they made it home safely.

Meanwhile back on the train, we all commented that The Way of the Roses route had been so picturesque and so well thought out, it was one of the better ones we'd undertaken.

Day 5: Tuesday

Bill delivered the bikes to my garage before the two of us returned the van to the Hertz depot. Over the next day or two, the riders popped round to reclaim their bikes.

3. Edinburgh to Liverpool

Background

The cycling tours I organised were becoming increasingly popular amongst my cycling chums, so much so that I was being asked to organise two tours a year. For this particular year, I planned the two routes in the shape of a cross. The Way of the Roses went from West to East and the Edinburgh to Liverpool route went from North to South. The two routes intercepted at High Bentham in Yorkshire.

I've mentioned that my mate, Roy, liked to start his tours from our homes in Wirral. For this one, I guessed he wouldn't mind too much if I arranged one which finished on Wirral instead.

As I regularly visit my relatives in Edinburgh, I knew the rough mileage was 260 miles which converted nicely into four cycling days of broadly 65 miles.

I began scouring OS maps and designed a route using local knowledge and a desire to ride over Eskdale Muir. Due to the remoteness of much of the route, it was important to choose sizeable towns at the right intervals for our overnight accommodation,

Fairly early on I decided that the legs would be:

- Edinburgh to Langholm (73 miles)
- Langholm to Kirkby Stephen (68 miles)

- Kirkby Stephen to Clitheroe (56 miles)
- Clitheroe to Liverpool (58 miles)

So a 255 mile tour, with a few extra miles to get us home from Liverpool.

After sending out my outline plan, sixteen signed up for it, plus Liz, who volunteered to drive a support vehicle. A great idea, as things turned out.

With no blue National Cycle Network signs to follow, I meticulously prepared route cards with turn by turn instructions highlighting which way to go at junctions and direction signs. The success of this method relied on careful comparison between the mileage on one's bike computer and the instruction on the route card at a given mileage. This was pre-Garmin. Thank goodness for modern technology.

People who wished to cycle free of luggage could have their bags carried in the support car.

Day 1: Friday daytime
During the day, riders made their own way to Edinburgh.

Five of us chose to add an extra day's cycling by taking our bikes by train from Liverpool to Glasgow and then cycling the 61 miles from Glasgow to the tour start in Edinburgh.

Fred and I opted to catch the 05.45 Liverpool/Glasgow train, arriving at 09.25 whilst Gary, Eddie and Dave caught a later Chester/Glasgow train.

The plan was for the five of us to ride in two separate groups along National Cycle Route 75 starting on the Clyde cyclepath and continuing through Coatbridge and Airdrie. Here we would join a new stretch of cycle path alongside the recently reopened railway line between Airdrie and Bathgate.

I'd also planned to call in to see my second cousin, Jimmy, who lives in Currie, on the outskirts of Edinburgh, and very near to the cycle route. Jimmy is an accomplished baker and his chocolate gateau is of upmarket tea room quality.

I think the folly of my Friday plan was threefold - (a) assuming that the signage would be 100%, (b) not having a back up means of navigation and (c) underestimating our likely speed of progress.

So, after a light breakfast I made my way to Fred's house for an 04.30 start. Having previously caught early trains, we knew the drill – a fairly easy ride through Birkenhead and the Mersey Tunnel to Liverpool Lime Street Station. Once on the station concourse, I was amazed to see so many commuters going off to work so early in the morning.

We changed trains at Manchester Piccadilly Station – a very busy junction. Here, we grabbed a coffee and a bun but our Lycra shorts felt conspicuously out of place in an ocean of suited businessmen and women crowding the platform.

Our connecting train was a disappointment. We're used to the comfort of a Virgin Pendolino, so this four-carriage diesel multiple unit felt a bit second rate. But we ticked along nicely and at 09.30 exited Glasgow Central Station ready to commence our ride.

Finding the River Clyde cycle path was easy and soon we were heading out of the city on this traffic-free route. At the six mile point we hit the first of many snags. We followed an NCR75 sign pointing across a footbridge and found ourselves in the Rutherglen area south of the river where there was no evidence of further signs.

When this happens it is always best practice to immediately stop and retrace ones steps. Maybe we were tired but, as is often the case, we fell into the trap of thinking that if we cycled just a bit further, then maybe a little more, we'd spy another sign.

The Sustrans "Forth and Clyde" map was too small a scale to be helpful so we reverted to asking passing strangers for assistance. I've found that generally, mature men and women with shopping bags, and taxi drivers, possess the least amount of knowledge regarding cycle paths.

It was lucky that a man on a mountain bike was able to tell us to ride back over the footbridge and to stay north of the river. I'd say we lost 30 minutes here all because of a vandalised sign pointing the wrong way, but I suppose someone must have found it hilarious.

Back on the riverside cyclepath we pedalled on for another ten miles reaching the town of Coatbridge. Once again the blue signs were confusing as they seemed to direct us up a ramp and into a covered shopping mall complete with an accordion playing busker. Surely that couldn't be correct. Fred and I turned our bikes around and made our way back to the road. We asked at a tyre depot for directions.

"Don't bother following the route", the chap said, "It's far too complicated. You're much better just riding on the road and picking up the cycle route on the other side of Airdrie". We followed his advice.

By now, I was becoming a little concerned about the time. A 9.30 departure to ride 61 miles with pannier bags was optimistic, but with two wrong turns plus frequent gate and anti-motor cycle barriers on the cyclepath, progress had been frustratingly slow.

Once past Airdrie, we found a park bench where we could eat our packed lunches before starting along a much better cyclepath next to the railway. As we approached Bathgate we came to a "path closed" sign with no obvious detour other than to ride into Bathgate itself. I think that was the last straw. It was now 3.30 and we had another 28 miles to cycle including a cake stop at Jimmy's house. It was time for a cup of tea and a rethink.

I had arranged a pre-tour drinks reception for 6pm prior to a meal booked for 7. As the tour's Head Prefect, and with some new riders to greet, I could not afford to arrive late. I reluctantly decided that Jimmy's chocolate gateau (another 18 miles or 90 minutes) would have to go, and that to make up time, we'd be best jumping on a train into Edinburgh.

I rang Jimmy to tell him the news. He was really disappointed, gutted even, and whilst two other relatives were in attendance, the prospect of eating their way through a massive chocolate gateau must have seemed daunting.

Fred and I finished our tea and made our way to Bathgate station where I was pleased to discover there is a frequent service to Edinburgh. We waited just 10 minutes and when we arrived at Waverley Station we spotted a number of our party arriving the sensible way.

Most of us were staying at the Travel Lodge in Rose Street. I had a massive room with power shower but was soon sprawled out on the bed grabbing a quick nap to catch up on lost sleep.

Day 1: (Friday) evening

My Scottish nephew had recommended the Thistle Bar in Rose Street as a meeting point. It was also convenient for our hotel. I met my cousin and his family just before six when the cycling group began dribbling in. I was catching up with my niece and my cousin's wife when Fred was overheard to say, "I can't believe Ian. He's only been in here 2 minutes and he's already chatting up those local women".

Nigel and Davy made a grand entrance dressed in loud Hawaiian shirts, shorts, sandals and sunglasses. I cringed when they loudly asked, "Where are the Jocks, then".

At 7.00 we walked around the corner to the Dogs Restaurant in Hanover Street, also recommended by my nephew. It was a great meal. While I was enjoying my main course Gary rang me to say that he, Eddie and Dave would definitely be joining us but they were running late.

During our pudding course they arrived at the restaurant.

After apologising for their late arrival, Gary asked me, "Did you and Fred have any problems with the route?"

"Yes, several"
"Did you follow that sign over the footbridge?"
"Yes"

"And did you pass the accordion player at Coatbridge?"

"Yes, him as well"

"And did you ride through the shopping precinct?"

"Err, no we passed on that one"

"And what about that diversion sign?"

"Yes, we obeyed that too"

But Gary told us that where Fred and I had given up, their trio had battled on, completing the 61 miles despite all of the setbacks. If I'd thought on, and given them Jimmy's phone number, they could have assisted with the demolition of the chocolate gateau too.

After returning to the hotel, I slept really well.

Day 2: Saturday – Edinburgh to Langholm

With an ambitious 73 mile leg to cover, I'd arranged for us to meet outside The Scottish Parliament building (near to Holyrood Palace and in the shadow of Arthur's Seat), for an eight o'clock start but there were two slippage incidents.

The first was slippage was caused by 16 riders trying to exit the hotel simultaneously using one puny lift. The second slippage was when we attempted to ride down the very greasy, and rain drenched, Royal Mile cobbles. Scary.

The delayed team photograph took place at 08.20 and soon after, we started our day's ride with a climb out of Holyrood Park.

A damp start from Holyrood Park

As the Travel Lodge did not provide cooked breakfasts, I'd arranged for us to call in at Morrison's three miles up the road. It was good to get out of the early morning rain. The breakfast was acceptable.

We resumed our urban ride south via Bonnyrigg and Gorebridge where we finally left civilisation to join the rural NCR1 and the very pleasant B7007.

The climb up the Moorfoot Hills was extremely character building as we battled into a headwind and driving rain. Even after crossing the watershed there was no respite in the weather and we still needed to pedal downhill to make progress.

I had booked tables for lunch at the Whistle Stop Café in Innerleithen, 30 miles from Edinburgh. This is a great cafe serving a menu of honest to goodness home cooking which is cooked to order. Unfortunately, touring cyclists do like to be in and out quickly, so sixteen riders arriving more or less together at premises already occupied by several "let's do lunch" families didn't help. Some riders became impatient and left to purchase sandwiches from the nearby Spar.

From Innerleithen we continued south on the beautiful and remote B7007 with many miles of silent roads enveloped by forest:

We rode passed the famous seismological station in Eskdale Muir before reaching the only opportunity for an afternoon refreshment stop at the Kagyu Samye Ling Tibetan Monastery.

Our visit to this haven of calm must rank as one of the highlights out of all of the tours I have completed.

The comfortable settees and naughty cake seemed at odds with a simple monastery life but we didn't ask too many questions.

The sugar boost certainly helped us to complete the final 15 miles into Langholm, a former textile town, christened "The Muckle Toon" for its population growth spurt and bustling mills, long since gone. The town was busy when we arrived, possibly because Manfred Mann were due to play in the Community Hall that evening.

I was in a B&B with Fred, who had found the day really tough. At age 81, he'd done well to ride 73 undulating miles in the rain, especially after our previous day's early start.

We had a quick shower and change before walking to our evening meal at The Douglas Hotel. At last the rain had gone off.

Another good night's sleep.

Day 3: Sunday – Langholm to Kirkby Stephen

We assembled at 09.15 in the small square in the centre of Langholm. The town was so quiet, a bit like Wirral during the 2020 Covid lockdown.

Today, Fred opted to ride in the support vehicle and nobody minded – he'd had a hard two days and deserved a break. But for the remaining cyclists, the route continued along delightful unclassified roads crossing the border into England before arriving in the lovely village of Brampton (at 22 miles) for a coffee stop.

More superb unclassified roads followed until we joined the picturesque Eden Valley. We continued to Langwathby (at 44 miles) for lunch in the Brief Encounter Tearoom at Langwathby Station. The tearoom was a fair

66

representation of the 1940's but fans of the Trevor Howard film would have been disappointed that the cafe had mysteriously relocated 50 miles north from Carnforth Station.

Appleby-in-Westmorland is an interesting town straddling the River Eden. It was not the right time of year for the annual horse fair so progress into the town was unhindered. At 55 miles, I'd earmarked a tea stop only to find the cafe had ceased trading so it was a case of a Mars Bar and water before we pressed on to our overnight stop in Kirkby Stephen.

We rounded off a great day's 68 mile cycle with a group evening meal at the Black Bull. Today marked Davy's wedding anniversary so we used the evening meal to help him to celebrate, along with his wife who had especially driven up from Wirral.

Day 4: Monday – Kirkby Stephen to Clitheroe

This was the toughest day of the tour so I had purposely kept the daily mileage down to 56.

We assembled at 09.15 in Kirkby Stephen's Market Square.

Our route continued along the Eden Valley but the initial gentle terrain did not properly prepare the troops for what lay ahead.

Crossing the Kendall/Northallerton road near to Hawes, we turned up the unclassified road towards Garsdale Head. Almost immediately we hit the long and steep, double chevron, climb up to Garsdale Common. One by one the riders dismounted and walked their bikes until the gradient eased. It was wild and beautiful on the top.

I knew from my End to End tour in 2007 that the descent from Garsdale to Cowgill was almost as steep. The speed of descent varied between those who had no fear and the more cautious riders amongst us. George is known within the group as "Gadget Man" as he has an array of the latest cycling accessories mounted on his bars. He was the only one in our group with a Garmin – an expensive piece of kit when first released.

As I was speeding down this long and fast descent and approaching Dent Station, I came upon George walking back up the hill. I pulled in to ask why.

He told me that his Garmin had just bounced out of its cradle. I looked at the long grass verges and thought, "No chance" before leaving him to his needle-in-a-haystack search and sped on down to meet the others at the foot of the descent in Cowgill. A few minutes later, a smiling George appeared, having miraculously located his Garmin in some long grass on the verge. Must have been his lucky day!

From Cowgill, we continued along the beautiful Dent Dale to the hamlet of Dent itself. I'd heard a lot about this quaint cobbled settlement and I was not disappointed.

Dent village

We were 20 miles into our daily mileage and with few opportunities for refreshments I'd earmarked Dent as a likely coffee stop.

Foolishly, I, and several others, stopped at the first premises with the word "coffee" displayed in the window. I say foolishly because not only was the coffee overpriced and terrible but more annoyingly because the machine had not been switched on and took forever to heat. Conversely, the remaining cyclists had continued round the corner to a delightful cafe for proper coffee and scones.

From Dent we travelled south on the unclassified road which climbs relentlessly 500 metres to a point to the west of Whernside – one of the Yorkshire Three Peaks. But I always say, the investment in climbing inevitably pays a dividend, usually stunning scenery. This was certainly the case as we sped downhill to Ingleton, another quaint village to the west of the second of the Three Peaks of Yorkshire – Ingleborough.

After a further four or so miles, we pulled in to High Bentham. Not only was this our lunch stop but it was also the point where we crossed our west to east "Way of the Roses" route earlier in the year.

From High Bentham there was more scenic climbing as we crossed into Lancashire and on to the top of the vast and remote Forest of Bowland. "Forest" is a misnomer as the bleak and treeless moors stretch as far as the eye can see in all directions:

We descended to Slaidburn, another small hamlet on the River Hodder and an opportunity for a cup of tea. After recommencing, I detected a peculiar metal-on-metal scraping noise coming from my rear derailleur. My gears had been "jumping" for much of the day, especially when engaging my lowest gear.

Our final 11 miles were not flat but the road gradually eased as we crossed the River Ribble into Clitheroe. I knew there was bike shop in Clitheroe and I promised myself an early morning visit the next day.

Our final meal of the tour was a disappointment. Having pre-booked a local pub, I was concerned to find just two members of staff on duty – one front of house and one in the kitchen. Their attempts to serve 16 three course meals from a ridiculously varied menu were clearly beyond them as they became totally stressed out. Two meals were returned and many of the remaining offerings left, part eaten.

I stayed overnight in the superb Brooklyn Guest House where I had a self contained holiday flat all to myself.

Day 5: Tuesday – Clitheroe to Liverpool

The team had been asked to assemble at 09.15 in the station car park. However, as I was taking my bike to the bike shop, I asked Roy to tell the others not to wait for me. I'd also asked Roy to ask Liz to hold the support car, just in case.

I was pleased when the shop opened on time. I wheeled my bike into the workshop expecting a quick tweak of the rear derailleur but the proprietor pointed out serious damage which I hadn't spotted. Not only had the teeth on the upper of the two small derailleur sprockets worn very badly, almost flat in fact, but my rear wheel had three broken spokes. The cause had been a worn chain which I had failed to replace. It was just as well I'd asked Ron to hold Liz and the support car. This would be a longer job than expected.

By 10.45, my bike had a new rear wheel, a new rear cassette, a new derailleur and a new chain. Oh, and I had a new, and large, bill to pay. By now I was too far behind to catch the group, Liz loaded my bike on to the bike rack and gave me a lift as we chased the group through Whalley and a minor road north of Blackburn to the coffee stop at The Top Lock - a canalside pub and tearoom near to Whittle-le-Woods. I'd missed out on 21 miles worth of up and down cycling and had to endure a lot of moans about the hilly route.

After coffee, it was good to be back on my bike especially as my gears were now changing like clockwork. It was a lesson learned and I now regularly use a chain checking tool.

After cycling a further 18 miles of typical Lancashire lanes we arrived at the Plough Inn, Euxton, for an alfresco lunch in a sunny beer garden. It is always hard to remount after a longish break but with just 18 miles to go, we set off down (now familiar) roads into Liverpool, pausing at the Pier Head for team photographs before saying our farewells and dispersing.

This had been a tough tour but very satisfying and we'd seen the very best of The Scottish Borders and Pennine England.

4. Isle of Man – The Lighthouses Challenge

Background

When our Edinburgh to Liverpool tour returned to the Pier Head, I was taken by the sight of the Isle of Man car ferry/catamaran sweeping majestically up the Mersey before berthing just 200 metres away.

Immediately, an idea for a Manx cycling weekend came to mind and I began planning.

The process inevitably starts with a map. But local knowledge is always helpful too so I contacted the local Manx cycling club to ask for ideas for day rides. I received a prompt and courteous reply from Steve who organises the annual **Lighthouses Challenge** – an out and back "sportif" with three distances to/from Douglas – 27 miles, 57 miles or 100 miles. It sounded ideal and after I described the abilities of our cycling group, he encouraged us all to participate.

The sportif description reads:

"For any cycling fans who haven't yet seen the breathtaking beauty of the Manx coastline for themselves, then we'd highly recommend building a cycling trip around this unique activity. Taking in a host of wildlife, rolling hills,

and even the possibility of witnessing basking sharks and dolphins close to shore, the Challenge truly offers a sight to behold while you pedal away.

The event is not for the faint-hearted, testing both endurance and stamina. But you do have a choice of three distances meaning you can select the one best suited to your cycling ability and fitness levels.

Starting at the famous TT grandstand in Douglas, the course runs around the Island's lighthouses and the spectacular coastline".

When I put the word out to the usual suspects, there was much interest. We ended up with 34 participants, mostly regular cyclists, some occasional cyclists and one or two non cycling partners. Here's what happened:

Saturday travel:

We travelled to Liverpool by local train. The designated meeting point was the Isle of Man ferry terminal, but there were one or two hiccups before we boarded.

Firstly, Bill left the train without realising he'd left his pannier bags on the train's luggage rack.

Then, I proposed a cup of coffee at a nearby cafe before boarding. It took so long to be served that my mobile phone kept pinging with, "Where on earth are you, Ian?" texts. A few burned gullets later, and we were all in the queue.

Finally as we started to move down the gangway to board, JIm asked me why I was clutching a white card. "Err, it's my boarding card – you have to get one from that office over there". Cue: The Roadrunner.

With all bikes safely stacked by the side of the car deck, we made our way to the passenger lounge to spread out for our three and a half hour voyage. The Irish Sea was as calm as a millpond and the group were clearly in a holiday mood. It was all very relaxed until Bill suddenly remembered where he'd left his pannier bags and started frantically planning a clothes raid on Marks and Spencer.

Arriving in Douglas, we had just over an hour to check in to our accommodation before meeting up for the first ride of the weekend.

Ride 1: The Laxey Wheel

This optional afternoon ride from Douglas to the Laxey Wheel and back was just 16 miles, with afternoon tea at The Old Corn Mill Cafe alongside the wheel.

This ride attracted a small group of about 10 riders who enjoyed the stunning coastal scenery along the cliff tops at Groudle Glen. They coped easily with the moderate climbs.

At the Laxey Wheel itself, we had plenty of time to view this enormous feat of engineering and take photographs before visiting the cafe.

Part way through our tea and scones, a second group arrived, some with novice partners in tow. They'd been late arriving for my 3pm departure and had watched despondently as they spied our yellow high-visibility jackets disappearing up and over Onchan Head. They were even more despondent when they discovered they'd arrived just too late for last orders at the cafe.

If my tight timetabling had made me unpopular, I was even more unpopular as I led the combined group of scone-sated and scone-less individuals up a very steep gradient to reach a mist covered *Social Cott.*

The descent to Douglas was fast and furious. We called in to the Lighthouses Challenge HQ to register for the next day's event. As we were being issued with our numbers, and complimentary goody bags, I began to feel uneasy as I looked around at the other participants and their bikes. My cronies did not seem uneasy though - they seemed so excited to be part of a mass participation ride.

Saturday evening

We all gathered in the hotel bar for pre-dinner drinks before moving through to the dining room. I say "all" but that wasn't really accurate. One of our party, who, for reasons of anonymity, I shall call Ben, was a member of a proper cycling club. He was by far the most experienced cyclist amongst us. In the past, he'd raced at a high level and his bike had to be seen to be believed. Ben had been so looking forward to riding the sportif with the best of the Manx riders.

When Ben and his wife failed to appear at dinner, I asked around and was shocked to hear that he was in Noble's Hospital, Douglas. Apparently, he'd earlier ridden with our second group up to the Laxey Wheel where his wheels became stuck in the tram lines. I don't need to complete what happened next, but luckily for Ben, he escaped with no fractures - just a very stiff shoulder, a few abrasions and I'm guessing, a huge dollop of "don't tell my cycling club" embarrassment. His biggest disappointment was that he was unfit to ride in the next day's event.

During the meal, Steve, the friendly Lighthouse Challenge organiser, popped in to say hello. I tried to brief him on the nature of our group - runners who are not really cyclists – but he did not seem bothered that many of us would find ourselves well out of our comfort zones.

His last words were, "I'll see you on the grid tomorrow"

Ride 2: Sunday – The Lighthouses Challenge

We assembled at the famous TT race grandstand, having collected our "dibbers" – electronic devices to provide proof that we had actually visited all of the lighthouses.

Within our party we had four riders aiming to complete the 100 miles; ten riders aiming to complete the 57 miles and ten to complete the 27 mile distance. I had undertaken to lead a small group of six novice riders on the 27 mile course. The remaining people did not participate due to injury or being non-cyclists.

On the grid, all of the other competitors seemed to be young, slim, and astride high-end road bikes. Some of our party had half decent bikes but there were many hybrids, or worse. We took our places at the back of the grid.

Right on time, Steve sounded the starting horn. As we passed him, he gave us all a loud and conspicuous welcome over the public address system.

During the first downhill mile into Douglas, my group of six was easily able to keep up with the tail end of perhaps 300 riders. Soon, however, we found ourselves totally dropped as we climbed sharply out of the capital and on to Douglas Head, joining the beautiful, and traffic free, Marine Drive.

We also became conscious that not only was our sextet isolated, but we were riding just in front of the broom wagon. After a couple more slow miles, we could no longer withstand the embarrassment and waved the broom wagon through.

I have to say that the organisation was exceptionally good. There were direction signs at every turn and smiling marshalls giving cheerful encouragement.

Looking across to Douglas from Marine Drive

The route was pretty too but a little lumpy as we passed through Port Soderick and Ballasalla. Eventually we arrived in Castletown – a really interesting place to visit, had we not been trying to beat out the miles. The first lighthouse on our list was at Dreswick Point, a mile or so south of Castletown. After some fumbling for dibbers we all managed to dib the machine and register our visit.

But the troops were revolting:

"When's the coffee stop?" I was asked.

"Coffee stop? What coffee stop?" I replied.

"We always have a coffee stop."

Blimey! How was I supposed to magic up a coffee shop in unfamiliar territory?

On our way back to Castletown from the lighthouse, I spotted a posh looking golf club. I was very tempted to knock on the door but I was very nervous having been mentally scarred by a previous golf club experience. During a "Coast and Castles" cycling tour with a family group, we were refused entry to a golf club in Northumberland due to the dress-code ban on shorts in the clubhouse. On that occasion, we were begrudgingly given tea in cardboard cups but were made to sit on a bench outside in a freezing easterly wind to drink it. After that episode, I held out little hope.

I tentatively knocked on the door, which clearly displayed the clubhouse dress code. Like the golf club in Northumberland, shorts were not allowed so what chance in our Lycra shorts?

The steward answered.

As politely as I could, I said "I realise we are not appropriately dressed for the clubhouse, but is there any chance at all that we could have a cup of coffee?"

"Of course, come on in", he replied smilingly.

The six of us were shown up to a sumptuous first floor members' lounge, not only with super-comfy leather settees but impressive panoramic views of the coast. The choice of coffees was as good as any upmarket Italian Bistro but the choice of cakes was even better.

It was so pleasant digging in to exceedingly large wedges of chocolate gateau and drinking good quality coffee as we thought of our chums who would, conversely, be digging in to the long climbs and longer miles ahead.

After a second round of coffees, guilt crept in and we decided we really ought to be moving on, so we thanked mine host for his excellent hospitality and attempted to continue with our Lighthouses Challenge. Unfortunately, all the direction signs had, by now, been collected and the marshalls stood down. I had attempted to memorise the route so we were able to find our way to Port St Mary and a really stiff climb up on to the 165 metre crag called, Cregneash.

The views from the top were stunning but the thoughts of riding all the way down to the Calf of Man lighthouse at sea level, dib dibbers, and then ride all the way back up the crag again was too much for most. Instead, Gary and I collected everyone's dibbers before making our descent.

The Calf of Man

It was a shame the others didn't pop down to see the spectacle of those raging waves as they roared through the Calf Sound. Six dibs later and Gary and I commenced our climb back up to rejoin the others. I was pleased the marshalls had left – I would not have liked it if our sextet had been disqualified on the grounds of multi-dibbing. Together we rode a steep descent into Port Erin and the official refreshment stop.

On arrival we were astonished to find that, like one of Tommy Cooper's illusions, the food had completely vanished, just like that. In fact, just like the disappearing signage and disappearing marshalls. The organisers had sent the remaining food on to the next feed station believing there could not possibly be any other riders still out there.

Port Erin marked the end of our 27 mile route so we made our way to the railway station to avail ourselves of the free transport back to Douglas on the delightful Victorian steam railway. What a treat this was clickety-clacking through the Manx countryside as we thought of our friends tackling their hilly routes.

On board the Manx Steam Railway

Sunday evening

Once again we gathered in the bar for pre-dinner drinks. Conversation was very animated as all had tales to tell.

Pete, one of our stronger riders had completed the 100 mile route but not without incident. Somewhere around the 65 mile point he'd buckled his rear wheel and in order for the wheel to turn unimpeded, he'd had to release his rear brake calliper. With some tidy climbs and fast descents, completing the ride with just a front brake and a buckled wheel was impressive.

Ally, another of our stronger riders had set off to do the 100 miles. Unfortunately for him, the 57 mile and the 100 mile courses shared the same feed station at St. John's but afterwards the two routes separated. Ally mistakenly followed some of our 57 milers out of the compound and did not realise his error until he'd covered too many miles to turn back. He was not best pleased.

Pete's wife, Jill, and cycling buddy, Ceri, were determined to complete the 100 mile route. It was a really, really, tough course but they had the grit to complete it, even though it was dark by the time they reached the finish. Well done!

Seven completed the 57 miler with various tales, including one broken chain. Three started the 57 miler but the grind up to St John's defeated them and they returned to join my group for the train assist back to Douglas.

Adam's efforts had left him so knackered that his pre-dinner snooze turned into a deep slumber. To avoid him missing his celebration dinner, the hotel staff had to almost batter the door down to rouse him.

Ride 3 Monday - Snaefell

After the previous day's exertions, it was no surprise that we had just four riders for the morning ride up the Isle of Man's highest peak – Snaefell. On a clear day there are spectacular views of the Lake District fells, Northern Ireland's Mountains of Mourne, and Snowdonia.

We left Douglas at 09.15 to ride the excellent B22 – a lovely route passing beautiful lakes and forests. There was a bit of harder climbing involved at *Injebreck Hill* where we came out of the tree line before a bit more climbing up to Bungalow Station.

Climbing up to Bungalow Station

From here, our plan was to walk the remaining half mile to the summit but with the route shrouded in mist I didn't fancy inadvertently finding the quick way down. We opted for the railway, paying £8.00 each for a 10-minute, totally mist-obscured ride up to the summit cafe. It was like being stuck in the ghost train, but without any ghosts. We met the non-cyclists for morning coffee.

After refreshments, the railway returned us to the Bungalow Station where we remounted and cycled the TT course back to Douglas – a very fast 8 mile descent.

Back in Douglas, we joined the others at the ferry terminal for our sail back to Liverpool.

What a great weekend.

5. Welsh Castles

Background

My mate, Roy must take the credit for thinking up this one. Did I already mention that he prefers to tour either starting from home, or finishing at home? Well, this one gave him the best of both worlds, starting <u>AND</u> finishing in Wirral.

During our programme of weekly rides, we had frequently visited the Edwardian castle at Flint and during a longer ride, Rhuddlan Castle, near Rhyl. Roy came up with the idea of cobbling together a tour to encompass all of the Edwardian castles which are dotted around the North Wales coast.

What are the Edwardian castles?

In 1277 Edward I launched an invasion of the native Welsh strongholds in North Wales, intending to establish his rule on a permanent basis. He instructed his nobles to construct eight new castles at Aberystwyth and Builth in mid-Wales plus Beaumaris, Conwy, Caernarfon, Flint, Harlech and Rhuddlan in North Wales. Additionally, he captured Criccieth Castle and remodelled it. Historian, Allen Brown has described these as "amongst the finest achievements of medieval military architecture in England and Wales".

This tour visited the seven North Wales castles in Harlech, Criccieth, Caernarfon, Beaumaris, Conwy, Rhuddlan and Flint.

After studying a few maps, I proposed four bite-sized cycling chunks:

Home to Bala (54 miles)
Bala to Porthmadog (58 miles)
Porthmadog to Bangor, via Beaumaris (47 miles)
Bangor to home via Conwy, Rhuddlan and Flint castles (73.5 miles)

Apart from the final day, mileages were kept low to take account of the hilly terrain and to allow time to view and photograph the castles.

By the starting date of the tour we had attracted a party of 18.

Day One: Friday, Wirral to Bala (54 miles)

The tour started at The Harp Inn - a remote hostelry situated on the banks of the River Dee in Little Neston, a former seaport for Dublin. The estuary is now silted up into a salt marsh covered with spartina grass. The excellent tarmac cycleway, built alongside the marsh in 2013, provides a traffic-free route between The Harp Inn and North Wales.

By starting the ride at 09.00, we factored in a slower rate of travel to take account of the day's climbs ahead.

The first part of the route was very familiar to our normal weekly ride participants. We crossed the River Dee into Wales using the boarded cycleway at the side of the railway bridge. Several stiff climbs later, we arrived at our coffee stop at the "eco" Caffi Florence within Loggerheads Country Park.

Those familiar with the area will know that at 554 metres, Moel Fammau is the tallest of the Clwydian Hills. As we left the coffee stop, I closed my ears to the moans once we immediately started climbing. At the Bwlch Penbarras cattle grid, just below the Moel Fammau summit we paused to take in the wonderful views of the Clwyd Valley and distant Snowdonian peaks.

Having ridden up to the Bwlch, we quickly descended the scarily steep lane complete with sharp hairpin bend, to the valley floor at Llanbedr where we joined the lumpy-in-parts B5429 south. Reaching the Dee Valley at Carrog, we were just in time to see and hear the steam powered passenger train (operated by the Llangollen Railway) make its wistful journey along the valley floor.

Shortly we arrived at our lunch stop at Corwen.

Following a sandwich lunch, our final leg flattened out as we cycled along quiet lanes, through limestone hamlets, to reach the tourist town of Bala. All eighteen had managed to find accommodation in various B&B's and had arranged to meet later for our evening meal together. As it was Friday, and as Bala has few eateries, I had taken the precaution of booking tables at the Plas yn Dre restaurant.

Roy and I were billeted in a B&B run by a former racing cyclist and his wife. Although long-retired, he took great delight in sharing his memories, and showing off his trophies, but we had a meal deadline to meet so left completion of our conversation until the morning.

The meal was convivial and the day's fresh air and exercise ensured my sleep quality was excellent.

Day two: Saturday, Bala to Porthmadog (58 miles)

We met at the TE Ellis statue in Bala's main street. (*Ellis was a locally born politician who was the leader of Cymru Fydd, a movement aimed at gaining home rule for Wales. He sadly died 1899 aged 40*).

And so we commenced day two, riding the quieter of the two roads on either side of Bala Lake, the largest natural body of water in Wales.

While on holiday, forty years previously, I had taken a pre-breakfast swim in the lake every morning, probably to try to impress my fiancée's family. It must have worked as we celebrate our golden wedding anniversary next year.

With lake views to our immediate right, the first few miles provided relaxed cycling. Was I the only one who knew that all would change soon?

At the southernmost end of the lake we crossed the A494 and began climbing what is often referred to as "The Military Road".

The Military Road

The occasional five barred gates not only retain flocks of sheep in their designated enclosures but they also deter motorised traffic from invading this delightful cycle route through the Snowdonia National Park. However, the freedom to cycle in absolute peace and quiet, in beautiful and remote countryside, comes at a price – a series of sharp and nasty climbs, even tougher with loaded pannier bags on board.

This superb route eventually turned south to take us through the equally stunning Coed-y-Brenin Forest. The long and gentle decent was overdue, taking us directly to our lunch stop in Dolgellau. Here the riders who had already arrived told us of an unnecessary altercation with the owner of a cafe who clearly preferred elderly couples to cyclists. We located a nearby pub serving tasty bar meals.

Leaving Dolgellau, we joined National Cycle Route 8 which meanders alongside the glorious Mawddach Estuary.

This stretch is frequently quoted in Sunday Supplements as a must do, eight mile, family ride. It is stunningly beautiful as the well surfaced cycle path along a former railway line hugs the estuary's bank before crossing a rickety railway bridge to Barmouth.

This brash, burgers and candyfloss, seaside resort came as a bit of shock after our previously rural scenery but we were soon clear, heading north to bag our first Edwardian castle at Harlech.

Harlech Castle *was completed by King Edward I in 1289 but suffered a chequered history thereafter. In 1404, it fell to Owain Glyndŵr but was recaptured in 1409. During the War of the Roses, it was held by the Lancastrians but was taken by the Yorkists in 1468. During the English Civil War, the castle was held by forces loyal to Charles I but was recaptured by Parliamentary armies in 1647. The 1468 siege is immortalised in the song, "Men of Harlech". Harlech Castle is a now World Heritage site.*

Whist enjoying a cup of tea and admiring the castle, some passing cyclists kindly warned us of a long diversion ahead. Our route would ordinarily have crossed the Afon Dwyryd using a toll bridge alongside the railway but the bridge was currently closed to traffic. This meant a ten-mile diversion to the next bridge upstream at Maentwrog,

To reach our overnight stop in Porthmadog, the party split three ways. Some boarded a train at Harlech Station for the short journey across the railway bridge to Porthmadog whilst others simply "dug in" and cycled the additional ten miles around the diversion.

The naughty group approached the closed toll bridge and discovered some scaffolding under the bridge, supporting some workmen's access planking. Despite evidence of security cameras, the naughty group (led by the rebellious Roy), wheeled their bikes along the planks and resumed their ride on the other side. There was never any comeback.

Apart from three campers, (Brrrr, in April!), the rest of our party were staying in a Travelodge. This would normally have been straightforward but two of our men, who were sharing a room, discovered they'd erroneously booked in for the previous night and this being Saturday it was no surprise that the hotel was fully booked. Adam kindly agreed to the receptionist's suggestion to split his double bed into two singles and to add a further temporary bed, at no cost.

That evening, we dined together at The Ship Pub, in Porthmadog.

Day three: Sunday, Porthmadog to Bangor, via Beaumaris (47 miles)

We cycled into Porthmadog town centre for breakfast.

Suitably fuelled, we gathered in the Tesco car park and left at 09.15 to ride just 5 miles to our next castle.

Criccieth Castle *was originally a native Welsh castle built by Llywelyn the Great but later modified Edward I in 1283. In 1294, the castle was besieged by Madoc ap Llywelyn but survived. In 1404, Welsh forces captured the castle under Owain Glyndŵr, tearing down its walls and setting the castle alight. Some stonework still show the scorch marks.*

After viewing from a distance, we continued through Llanstumdwy village, the birthplace of David Lloyd George, the last Liberal Party leader to be a

119

British Prime Minister. Here we joined the excellent Lon Las Trail (National Cycle Route 8). Since we last rode it a few years previously, the surface had been upgraded to tarmac and progress was brisk.

As Roy's wife had been born in these parts, Roy had much local knowledge. He'd recommended that we approach our next castle, Caernarfon, from a seaward direction. This was really good advice as we diverted to a traffic-free coast-hugging minor road two and half miles shy of Caernarfon. The views as we approached the castle were spectacular. But Roy's chosen route was also totally exposed to a fierce headwind coming at us down the Menai Strait. Those last two and a half miles were really hard work.

With 28 miles completed, we tarried in Caernarfon's Castle Square where we enjoyed a light lunch sitting in the sunshine and admiring the impressive castle walls in front of us.

Caernarfon Castle was built by Edward I in 1283. The town and castle acted as his administrative centre for North Wales and as a result, the defences were built on a grand scale. But like the others, the castle had a chequered history. In 1294, Madog ap Llywelyn's forces sacked the castle but it was recaptured in 1295. In the English Civil War, it was held by Royalists. In 1911, Caernarfon Castle was used for the investiture of the Prince of Wales, and again in 1969. It is a World Heritage Site.

Following our lunch break, we continued along the Lon Las Trail, dropping our pannier bags off at our hotel, The

Premier Inn, Bangor, before crossing the Menai Bridge to the Isle of Anglesey and a six mile ride to Beaumaris, the only Edwardian castle never completed.

Beaumaris Castle's *construction was delayed due to lack of funds and work only began in 1295. Edward's invasion of Scotland diverted funding and work stopped completely, only recommencing in 1306. When work ceased around 1330 the castle remained incomplete.*

During the English Civil War, the castle was held by forces loyal to Charles I, holding out until 1646 when it surrendered to the Parliamentary armies. The castle fell into ruin around 1660. It is currently managed by Cadw as a tourist attraction.

After our visit we made our way back over the Menai Bridge to our hotel for our evening meal.

Day four: Monday, Bangor to home (73.5 miles)

Leaving the Premier Inn at 09.15 we rode through the city of Bangor to reach the National Cycle Network Route 5. The cyclepath and minor roads were excellent to begin with but during one scary part, the route had us cycling against the traffic on a cycle lane simply painted onto the busy A55. I hope this has since been changed.

Someway before Penmaenmawr we left the A55 to cycle an interesting mix of rural lanes and civil engineering solutions to guide us around a headland and on to the riverside quay at Conwy. With 21 miles on the clock, it felt like coffee time. We found an interesting cafe with a rooftop terrace where we could enjoy views of the castle, the

Conwy Estuary and the associated quayside activity.

Conwy Castle was built between 1283 and 1289 as part of a larger project to create the walled town of Conwy. It too had a mixed history. In 1642, it was held by forces loyal to Charles I during the English Civil War but in 1646 was recaptured by a Parliamentary Army. In 1665, the castle was stripped of iron and lead and left to ruin, but in the late 18th century, it became an attractive destination for painters. In the 19th century, visitor numbers grew and some restoration work was carried out. The castle is currently managed by Cadw as a tourist attraction.

After coffee, our route crossed the River Conwy and on reaching Colwyn Bay we followed Route 5 along the succession of seaside promenades and static caravan parks to the once thriving holiday town of Rhyl where we took the inland cyclepath to Rhuddlan castle.

Rhuddlan Castle, next to the River Clwyd, was completed in 1282. During the fortification's lengthy construction, the river course was altered to allow ships to sail inland along a man-made channel. Its purpose was to allow provisions and troops to reach the castle even if hostile forces or a siege prevented overland travel.

Rhuddlan Castle was garrisoned by Royalist troops during the English Civil War. It was taken by Parliamentary forces after a siege in 1646. Two years later, the Parliamentarians partially demolished the castle to prevent any further military use.

Cycling from Rhuddlan we had a choice of routes to Flint and our final castle of the tour. The coastal route is flat and there are plans to convert an existing coastal footpath into a traffic-free cycle route. At the time of writing, the flat route currently utilises the A548. The alternative is to head up and over the hills from Gronant on National Cycle Network Route 5. This is an extremely pleasant route with extensive views all along the Halkyn Mountain ridge.

With a day's cycling total of 73 miles, we decided to leave the hillier route for another day and opted for the coastal route. We paused at the excellent Nant Hotel, Prestatyn, for an al fresco sandwich lunch. From here it was a case of heads down for 12 miles along the A548, though there are several points where the traffic leaves the old road on a modern bypass leaving sleepy villages for peaceful cycling.

Soon, we were in Flint and at our final castle.

The castle was the first to be built by Edward I and completed in 1286, with a tidal moat. The site is in a strategic position, just one day's march from Chester, and supplied via the River Dee. The design of Flint Castle was not repeated and its layout remains unique within the British Isles. In 1399 Richard II of England was held in the castle by Henry Bolingbroke. During the English Civil War it was held by the Royalists but captured by the Parliamentarians in 1647 and "sllghted" in accordance with Cromwell's destruction order. The ruins are what remain today.

After a brief stop we continued on National Cycle Route 5 as far as Connah's Quay and our ride home back across the River Dee using the railway bridge.

The tour had been a great success. Tough, yet educational and with few mishaps.

6. The Outer Hebrides

Background:

In 2014, I organised a tour of the Outer Hebrides from South to North.

It would have been a huge success except for the weather which was particularly unkind that year. After completing our first day, taking in the islands of Vatersay, Barra and South Uist, the next day saw us attempting to cycle into a fierce and cold headwind, accompanied by driving rain.

After an hour, we'd covered just 6 miles. Adam and I had been dropped by the rest of the group and I was beginning to feel hypothermic. I realised that with a further 54 miles to go, we would not make sufficient progress to reach our ferry connection over to Harris.

I knew there was a bike hire business nearby, with possible bike transport, so called into a remote haulage business to seek directions. Adam and I were dripping water all over the reception floor as we received the news that the bike hire man was away on holiday.

Plan B was to ask if they had any transport going north with which we could grab a lift but they all had already left. My final option (Plan C) was to ask if we could hire a van.

"Aye", said the chap in reception, "I'll just ring my boss".

He returned to say, "Yes, that's fine". It would be £70. (Not bad, I thought).

"Oh, and then there's the fuel". (Still fine, I thought).

"Oh, and then we'd need to send two men in a vehicle to retrieve the van from the ferry terminal, so how about £100?"

To be honest, I was so cold and wet I would have paid £100 just for myself, so split between the group that sounded like a reasonable deal. Besides, our negotiating position was nil!

I counted out £100 in £20 notes and we were handed the keys. As an afterthought he said, "You do have driving licences, don't you?" Neither of us had them with us so we just nodded and we were on our way.

We threw our bikes in the back of the van and drove after the others with the heater on full blast. First, we caught a shivering but enormously grateful Andrew who couldn't believe his luck. Once on board we caught the others and they all piled in.

The only place open for a lunch stop was a fairly posh hotel but we had no qualms about parking the van in their car park and parking ourselves in their lounge where we ordered hot soup. I am a vegetarian and the soup of the day was pea and ham, but do you know what? At that moment I wouldn't have cared if it had been Aberdeen Angus stew.

Gradually we thawed out but, despite valiant attempts with the hand dryers in the toilets, our clothes never fully dried out.

But we did make it to the ferry where we handed over the keys to the lads who'd arrived to collect the van. We crossed to Harris to continue our disappointingly wet tour.

Once home, I vowed not to waste all of my tour planning. I undertook to nail the tour properly by organising an identical trip for the following September. This is what we did in 2015:

Travelling North:

There were six in the party.

We met at Glasgow Queen Street Station for the train to Oban. Anyone who has used this service will know that the train crew take the cyclists through the barrier first so that bikes may be loaded before the other passengers. We had booked all six bike spaces for our six bikes. While we were loading our bikes onto the train, a seventh cyclist appeared.

In a "more than my job's worth" moment, the conductor would not allow him to board, despite the man's pleas that he needed to connect with the ferry to Barra that afternoon. He added that he had a bed booked at the Castlebay hostel. We left him on the platform as the train pulled out.

After a three-hour train journey, admiring fabulous scenery, we arrived in

Oban. At the CalMac ferry terminal, we purchased discounted "Hopscotch 8" tickets to cover our four ferries:

- Oban - Castlebay (Barra)
- Barra - Eriskay
- Berneray – Leverburgh (Harris)
- Stornoway (Lewis) - Ullapool

Boarding was easy and at 15.40 we departed for one of the finest ways to start a Hebridean holiday. Sailing through the beautiful Sound of Mull, we were accompanied by a large school of dolphins. We had a tasty meal on board and docked at Castlebay, Barra, just as the sun was setting.

I do like my home comforts so I'd booked in to the Castlebay Hotel whilst the other five were in the Dunard Hostel.

Day 1:
At 09.15 I met the others outside their accommodation.

"You could have stayed with us, Ian", one of them said. "There was an empty bed with a card on it which said, 'Mr Noon' ". We knew immediately who this was referring to. (Incidentally, when I heard this, it struck me that Mr. Noon must be the only person I know whose name reads the same forwards as backwards).

We left Castlebay and rode south across the causeway to cross to the most southerly of the inhabited Outer Hebridean islands - Vatersay. Riding on empty single track roads was bliss.

Just above the shoreline, we stopped to view the preserved remains of a World

War II Catalina aircraft which crashed in 1944. We spent a few minutes thinking about the crewmen who had died and whose names are on a memorial nearby. We continued to the most southerly point at Bhatarsaigh where there are views across to Sandray, Pabay, and Mingulay (as in "The Mingulay Boat Song").

On our return we paused at Siar Bay – the most beautiful beach I have ever encountered. The bay is on the opposite side of the narrow isthmus to the Catlina site and is marked with a stone monolith. Here, we gazed at the bright turquoise sea washing over almost a mile of pure silver sand.

Despite it being September, the breeze was warm. Two of us walked through the sand dunes to reach this totally deserted beach where we spontaneously stripped off and ran into the Atlantic Ocean. Yes, it was cold but after a few strokes the body soon acclimatises. Emerging from the waves we ran the length of the beach to allow the breeze to dry our skin. It felt totally natural and I still find it hard to fully describe the immense feelings of liberation, exhilaration and sheer joy. Finally we pulled our cycling kit back on to our dry bodies and rejoined the others.

Our ride continued back over the causeway and along the western edge of Barra to the air terminal – the only one in the UK where scheduled flights land on the beach.

We continued north to Eolaigerraidh Cemetery to look for the grave of Compton McKenzie, author of "Whisky Galore" – the story of the wreck of The SS Politician on Eriskay and its cargo of whisky finding its way into the homes of the locals.

According to Wikepedia:

*The **SS Politician** was a cargo ship that ran aground off the coast of the Hebridean island of Eriskay in 1941. Her cargo included 22,000 cases of malt whisky. Much of the whisky was recovered by islanders contrary to marine salvage laws. Because no duty had been paid on the whisky, members of HM Customs and Excise pursued and prosecuted those who had removed the cargo.*

Bottles of whisky have since been raised from the seabed by divers, and some have been found in hiding places on Eriskay. The story of the wreck and looting was the basis for the book Whisky Galore; an adaptation was released as a film in 1949 and a remake in 2016.

Back at the airport, we lunched in the coffee shop which is highly recommended, before witnessing the

Glasgow fight coming in to land on the sands.

I think the pilot's name was Sandy

Our ferry to Eriskay departed at 15.45 and after a 40 minute crossing we arrived at "Charlie's Bay" where Bonnie Prince Charlie landed to lead the 1745 rebellion.

The climb from the ferry is chain-snappingly steep and comes far too soon after 40 minutes of inactivity but it is over with reasonably quickly and from the top, there are great views of the bay below. Further down the road, we called in at the Politician Pub, named after the famous shipwreck. It would have been rude not to sample a whisky or two and to view some bottles salvaged from the original 1941 cargo.

We crossed another causeway (built 2000) looking out for otters before landing on South Uist and our overnight stop in Dalabrog. Once again, I opted for comfort at the Borrodale Hotel whilst the other favoured the Uist Bunkhouse.

Day 2

Leaving Dalabrog fairly early we had the benefit of a superb and warm tail wind which meant we were bowling along at 22 mph with little effort.

At the village of Howmore (Tobha Mor), I paused to call in to the haulage depot where our Good Samaritan from the previous year had come to our rescue. I was pleased to recognise Ian, the chap who'd been on duty that day. I reminded him of our previous visit and he did remember us. I thanked him for his helpfulness and trust that day before resuming our wind assisted ride.

Shortly, I spied another cyclist in front and recognised the chap who had been left on the train platform in Glasgow, a day or two previously.

"Hi. Are you Mr Noon?" I asked. He nearly fell off his bike with surprise. He must have wondered if I had some strange Mystic Meg powers. But he was OK after I'd explained that we were the ones on the station platform. He'd had to take a later train and travel over to the islands a day later. He was touring on his own, which must have been lonely. We discussed other tours we'd each completed and as we parted company, he recommended that we try Mull.

We were able to wear summer cycling clothing in the warm and balmy temperatures. It was such a contrast to the previous year when I missed out on seeing large swathes of island scenery by being in the back of a Luton van.

We cycled across yet another causeway on to Benbecula and paused at the town

144

of Benbecula itself for lunch. Thereafter, we made excellent progress on to North Uist where we had more than enough time to explore the 3000BC, and well preserved, megalithic tomb before heading for the remote ferry terminal at the north of the island.

The ferry departed at 17.20. On board, we were most surprised to find a plaque commemorating its construction by McTay Marine Limited – a small ship building yard on the banks of the Mersey very near to our homes back in Wirral. Sadly, the yard has been long closed.

After an hour's sail, we arrived at **Leverburgh**, on the island of Harris.

And here is yet another link with Wirral. Between 1964 and 1980, I worked for

Unilever in Wirral's Port Sunlight Village. Lord Leverhulme was the founder of Lever Brothers which later became the conglomerate, Unilever.

Unilever is perhaps most associated with Sunlight and Pears Soaps, Persil and Omo washing powder, Stork Margarine, Walls Ice Cream, Birds Eye fish products and many other well known brands.

In 1919, the first Lord Leverhulme had purchased the South Harris estate for the sum of £36,000. He planned to turn the hamlet of Obbe it into a consolidated major fishing centre, with products distributed through his Mac Fisheries shops.

*In 1920, the hamlet of Obbe was pompously renamed **Leverburgh,** and 300 men started work on a new pier and seashore infrastructure for processing* the seafood from 50 berthed trawlers. Shore construction included an accommodation block, curing sheds, smoke houses, a refrigeration building, store sheds and houses for the managers.

With a second stage of development planned to convert the inner sea loch into a harbour, Leverhulme paid for upgraded roads to accommodate the additional traffic. During his last visit to Leverburgh in 1924, Leverhulme developed pneumonia. After his death, the board of Lever Brothers had no interest in the project and so ended all work, selling off the village and production facilities for £5,000. It is estimated the project cost Leverhulme £500,000.

I stayed overnight at the excellent Caramish House, leaving the others to bed down at the Ambothan Bunkhouse. With limited eating facilities in

Leverburgh, we'd reserved a table at the Anchorage restaurant which serves seafood as a speciality.

Day 3

After a 9.15 start from the pier, we made our way to the 16th century St Clement's Church at Rodel. The church is open to view and contains many ancient wall carvings and tombs and was well worth our visit.

148

We cycled the single track road along the eastern side of Harris called, "The Golden Road" on account of the massive cost of construction in the 1930's. It is a great road to ride with its spectacular switchbacks dipping down to small fishing piers and then up and over headlands again.

The Golden Road

The Skoon Art Cafe part way along has the best homemade scones for miles.

Continuing around the coast, the road passes the Harris Tweed and Knitwear Exhibition Centre at the small community of Drinishader. It is well worth a visit, if only to try on the Harris Tweed jackets.

And so the Golden Road eventually joins the main road to Tarbet before dropping steeply to the port. Here we located a good cafe to take on sustenance ready for what lay ahead!

Soon after leaving Tarbert on the A859, the road rises steeply on a long and steep 1 in 6 gradient (15%). The climb was tough with pannier bags and two of us felt no disgrace in walking the steepest section.

Once on the top, we enjoyed a spectacular and undulating ride with much to see including the Harris hills to our left and Loch Seaforth to our right.

On our previous trip we stayed overnight at Stornoway but this time chose the Loch Erisort Hotel a few miles south of Stornoway. What a curiosity. The proprietor seemed to do everything – receptionist, barman, and chef. He showed us to our rooms in what looked like a 1970's modern extension. The en-suite bedrooms were massive. My only disappointment came when Ned ran the first bath and pinched every last litre of hot water. He was very apologetic.

Day 4

Today's ride was all about historic Lewis.

After leaving our hotel we cycled northwest to the spectacular Callanish

Stones and visitor centre. More impressive than Stonehenge and totally accessible, this stone circle is mesmerising. One could easily spend a half day here.

The atmospheric Callanish Stones

The visitor centre was very informative and the cafe excellent.

Just a few miles further north we took a slight detour to visit the Broch at Tolastadh. This defence tower and accommodation block dating back a number of years BC is damaged yet still a fine example of this design. It is definitely worth exploring.

The ruined Broch

And so our history tour continued as we cycled on to the Blackhouse Village at Garenin.

The "Blackhouse Village" consists of nine restored traditional thatched cottages which were lived in until 1974 and were the last group of blackhouses to be inhabited in the Western Isles.

In 1989, the Garenin Trust was established to restore the houses. A decade later the project was complete and the restored Blackhouse Village was opened by Princess Anne.

The Blackhouse Village – well worth a visit

As well as four self-catering cottages, there is a museum (a blackhouse set in 1955) with tweed weaving demonstration, and a café, where we enjoyed a superb lunch. The village recently featured in an episode of "Call the Midwife".

At this point we had a choice of continuing 32 miles north to The Butt of Lewis, then back again to Stornoway – a round trip 56 miles, or a direct route across Lewis to the capital. We'd spent just a bit too long admiring Hebridean history to allow sufficient time to make the Butt and back. Also, having had the benefit of a strong tail wind so far, this would have converted to a strong headwind for our return from the Butt.

Instead, we again returned to the ghost of Lord Leverhulme and rode the 17 mile Pentland Road between the Blackhouse Village and Stornoway. Originally laid out by Leverhulme's company as a railway to connect the west coast fishing villages with Stornoway, it is now a quiet single track road facilitating a direct return to the capital.

In some respects we found the road a remote and quiet oasis but in others, it was a long, straight and featureless drag, leaving us begging for a sight of Stornoway's outskirts.

And so to our final night on the islands. Whilst exploring Stornoway, I called in to the tourist office and in true Professor Higgins style, was astonished to hear what I correctly took to be a Wirral accent. Alastair, the receptionist, had previously worked for Wirral Borough Council before leaving to join both the Church of Scotland and the Stornoway Tourist Office.

We enjoyed an excellent curry at one of the local hotels near to the harbour. As usual, I stayed in an en-suite room in a guest house whilst the others opted for the Laxdale Bunkhouse.

Travelling home

I really enjoy cycling in quiet and remote corners of our isles but tours such as this require a big time commitment travelling there and back and this trip was no exception. We'd decided to tackle the Stornoway to Wirral journey in one go – tiring, but no overnight involved. My mate, Roy, would not have enjoyed this part.

Here's what we did:
We were all up very early in order to catch the ferry's check-in which closed at 06.15. With bikes stored, the ferry sailed at 0700, but the best bit was when the dining room opened and we gorged ourselves on full Scottish breakfasts all round.

After arriving in Ullapool at 09.45, reassuringly, I could see Nigel from Highland Cycle Transport waiting for us with his 12 seat taxi and trailer. We had used Nigel previously and he efficiently loaded the bikes, bags, and finally us, before setting off along picturesque roads to Inverness. During the journey he recounted his links with the Royal family.

At Inverness, we had plenty of time to purchase picnic lunches before boarding our train to Edinburgh. So far, so good, but, as Nat King Cole once sang, "There may be trouble ahead".

Our Edinburgh bound train was making good progress until there was a long delay at a junction whilst waiting for another train to pass. We were due to arrive at 16.22 in time for our connection to the 16.52 train from Edinburgh to Preston.

Our train conductor advised that we would not arrive in Edinburgh in time for our connecting train. He advised us to alight at Edinburgh Haymarket, (the station before Edinburgh Waverley) to connect with our train going south.

At Haymarket we waited three minutes before our Preston bound train arrived. I asked a member of the platform staff where the bike compartment was likely

160

to be. Incredibly, he replied that we were not permitted to board with bikes at Haymarket.

I approached the train manager. He explained that due to the excessive length of the train, the bike compartment was in the tunnel and could not be accessed. I explained that we had both seat and bike reservations and offered two solutions – loading the bikes into the empty disabled bay opposite but moving them to the bike compartment at the next stop; or walking the bikes down the train to the bike bay in coach A. Both of these suggestions were rejected outright.

In frustration, I boarded the train and placed my bike in the vast disabled bay. The train manager asked the platform attendant to call the police. Despite a fractious exchange, we finally convinced the train manager that we were acting on information given to us in good faith and that we did possess bike reservations on his train. He eventually allowed us on board and the police call was cancelled.

It turned out to be a long day of travelling, with two further trains – Preston to Liverpool and Liverpool to Wirral.

Since that experience, future tours have included stopovers.

Summary:

Despite the train problem, it was great tour and I am so pleased I decided to repeat our previous washout. Our post-ride reports did not go down too well with the group who had received their soakings the previous year. The weather definitely made a huge difference.

Recommended.

7. The Isle of Wight Randonnee

Background:

My wife and I attended a superb Christmas party where I was introduced to Jack, the father of the host. Jack was a similar age to me, and we had cycling in common, so it was an obvious pairing.

Jack had travelled to Wirral from his home on the Isle of Wight and once we engaged in serious discussion of all things cycling, it wasn't surprising to see my wife Chris, drift off to locate the cheese board.

After we'd talked gear ratios and bike frames, Jack enthusiastically described an annual cycling event back home - "The Isle of Wight Randonnee". He told me it has been around for over 30 years and is run over a choice of two distances – 34 miles or 62 miles. He added that it takes place on open roads but is not a race, more of a 3000-cyclist mass participation event.

After the success of our Isle of Man weekend, this sounded like a great way to see another of my previously unvisited British islands as well as exploring unfamiliar roads. I was hooked and commenced my planning.

After initial enthusiasm from my cycling chums, thoughts about complicated journeys there and back resulted in a gradual loss of interest until just my wife and I remained the last riders standing. We decided to make it a bit of a holiday and booked four nights in a hotel at the island's capital, Newport.

Travel to the Isle of Wight

As my mate, Roy, knows, travelling to far flung places with a bike can be problematical. I explored and then discounted the use of trains, so it came down to a 250 mile drive to Southampton and then a ferry across The Solent.

I packed the car the night before – two partly dismantled bikes inside to reduce wind resistance, and to avoid any risk of depositing them on the middle carriageway of the M6. We left early taking alternate one-hourly driving shifts and arrived at the Red Funnel Ferry terminal, Southampton, by 2.30.

Boarding was a piece of cake and after a smooth crossing we disembarked at East Cowes before driving to our accommodation at Newport and reassembling the bikes.

Pre-Randonnee

On our first morning, we took an exploratory ride along the banks of the River Medina up to Cowes. It wasn't "Cowes Week" but there was plenty of evidence of nautical money. A friendly cyclist who lived in the town told us what to look out for and, for our coffee break, suggested a bistro further around the coast. After taking various photographs in Cowes, we continued to Gurnard Bay and the excellent Waters Edge Cafe overlooking The Solent. After coffee in the sunshine, we cycled inland riding along a delightful road through Parkhurst Forest at the back of

Parkhurst Prison. The road eventually led us back to Newport and our hotel.

We'd arranged to meet Jack for afternoon tea in order to discuss arrangements for the next day's Randonnee. Jack had told us that riders can start the event at any of the six checkpoints dotted around the island. His recommendation was for the three of us to meet at The Wootton Bridge registration point which was conveniently midway between his house and our hotel.

We also discussed the weather forecast. We'd all seen the predictions for a fierce anti-cyclone travelling across the southern part of the island from around noon the next day. Jack asked me what I wanted to do if the weather turned really nasty. My answer was easy –

having endured many tour soakings, and with a warm hotel nearby, I would be aborting my Randonnee. A sense of relief came over Jack's face. He was 70 and I was 69 – too long in the tooth for heroic monsoon cycling.

The Randonnee
Sunday morning came and Chris and I were both up early for a full English breakfast to fuel our leg muscles.

We set off on our four mile warm-up ride to the Wootton Bridge checkpoint. Out on the road, there were many other cyclists including young families, serious club riders and everything in between.

There was certainly a buzz of anticipation at the registration point. Jack was easy to spot. He was riding a vintage road bike with frame-mounted shifters. He was also proudly sporting his Vectis Cycling Club jersey and cap. The island's Vectis Cycling Club was formed in 1883 but sadly had folded the previous year in 2016, due to member apathy.

It's always exciting to be given a number to tie on to the front of your bike and soon the trio of Jack, Chris, and I, was off following the clearly visible direction signs and being cheered on by friendly marshalls. I was amazed how many of them knew Jack as we rode a really interesting and traffic-free route through Nettlestone to the next check point at Bembridge. There were about 70 bikes parked outside.

We entered one of those 1940's community halls, a bit like the one in "Dad's Army". It had trestle tables at one end sagging under the weight of sandwiches and cakes. It was also alive with excited chatter.

The three of us squeezed up to a small table and Jack described the next part of the route. It was so kind of him to act as our personal escort when he could otherwise have been cycling with his Vectis chums.

Suitably refreshed, we remounted and continued to Alverstone. Here, Chris left us to return along the shorter 34 mile route back to Newport. She later told me that it was a delightful ride along the path of a disused railway. She was not cycling alone as there were many family cycling groups on that section too.

Soon after leaving Alverstone, I felt a few spits and spots of rain. The rate and size of the raindrops increased in direct proportion to the nearness we got to the next checkpoint at Ventnor Rugby Club, at which point the rain was simply biblical.

As we rolled into the compound we were approached by a man with a notebook and a large camera around his neck. He was from the local newspaper and was clearly seeking some ancient riders for his story, possibly headlined, "Never too old to ride the Randonnee". He took our photograph and interviewed Jack, who had entered every Randonnee since its inception.

After grabbing a cup of tea we popped back outside into torrential rain and a strong wind. We managed to find a gazebo to shelter beneath but after waiting for the best part of an hour, the storm showed no signs of abating. We looked at each other and knew immediately what the other was thinking.

I was lucky that having a local as my riding companion meant that he could take the most direct route back to Newport. It was case of rain jackets on and heads down as we battled across the island into a strong headwind and lashing rain. Initially our route followed the Randonnee as far as a hamlet called Whitwell. Here we ignored a signed left hand turn and continued for a few miles in a northerly direction. Further on, at Rookley, we paused for a quick nose blow and were astonished to see eight riders pull in behind us, all with Randonnee numbers on their bikes.

"Have you retired, too?" Jack asked them.

They looked confused.

"Retired? No, we're following you. Isn't this the Randonnee route?"

Oh, dear, the eight riders were by now in the centre of the Island, soaked, and several miles off course. Jack gave them verbal and complicated directions which would see them back on track but I would not have liked to have tried to memorise them.

With soaking wet gloves, socks and shoes, I decided to telephone Chris to ask her to run a hot bath. After another half hour, I was back at the hotel, totally wet through. I thanked Jack as he rode off to his home eight miles away before I

173

drip dripped my way to our room for a long and sudsy soak.

I asked Chris about her ride. "Fine", she replied, "No rain".

Monday sightseeing

After the previous day's stormy ride, I didn't want to see my bike again for at least a week. Instead, Jack had kindly offered to spend the day with us walking and sightseeing.

After breakfast, he appeared. The sun was shining and the wind had completely disappeared. Jack drove us to Yarmouth. We started on a delightful walk through Fort Victoria Country Park and on the coastal path around Warden Point to The Needles Visitor Centre. Judging by the coach and car parks, it didn't appear that many of the visitors had walked there.

The Needles

After several photographs at The Needles, Jack's route took us along the cliff tops and up to Tennyson's Monument standing on the highest point of the long chalk ridge – it is an imposing memorial to Alfred Lord Tennyson. Built in 1897, the views over land and sea were superb. Apparently,

Tennyson and his wife, Emily, lived in nearby Freshwater for thirty-nine years.

With "The Charge of the Light Brigade" ringing in my ears, our walk circled several leagues, several leagues, several leagues onward back to Jack's car. From here, he commenced an informed and exclusive tour of the island. The drive followed the Randonnee route in reverse and as we drove along the very exposed coastal/cliff road between the Needles and Ventnor, I knew we had made the correct decision to abort our ride the previous day.

Back at our hotel, Jack joined us for a cup of tea before we offered our profuse thanks for his excellent hospitality and said our farewells.

Aftermath:

Our ferry crossing and drive home were smooth and uneventful. A few days later, Jack sent me a copy of the local newspaper. In it was a two-page Randonnee special supplement. There were several photographs of lashing rain and soaking wet riders. Our picture was in there too with a piece about how the event attracts riders of all ages. It praised the couple of old relics who had completed The Randonnee in such appalling conditions, but we knew differently.

8. Mull and Iona (The "Four Islands" Tour)

Background:

It's funny how you engage strangers in conversation during cycling trips.

As mentioned earlier, during our Hebridean cycling holiday we encountered a solo cyclist with the palindromic surname, Mr. Noon. In conversation, we asked where else he'd cycled and if there was anywhere he would recommend. His unwavering reply was, "Mull", though he had warned us that it is very hilly.

Thus began more research into the possibilities of another Scottish tour.

Having read up and consulted maps it became apparent that the geography lent itself more to a single centre cycling holiday, (rather than a point to point tour), with added non-cycling activities to add variety.

And so our "Four Islands" holiday was born.

Access and logistics

The ferry to Mull leaves from Oban, so the first thing to arrange was travel to this picturesque Scottish port and the gateway to the islands.

Of the eight who signed up for the holiday, one couple, (Liz and George) drove their campervan from Wirral to the ferry. Andrew and Jim left Wirral at 06.00 and drove to Oban leaving their car in a long stay car park. Lynda travelled to Oban by train and caught a later ferry all in the same day.

The remaining trio of Ned, Tom and I cycled 44 mainly traffic-free miles from Wirral to Preston, to catch a Glasgow train before a relaxing overnight stop in the city. The following day, the three of us took the Oban train on one of the most scenic of Scottish railway lines.

We met Jim and Andrew in Oban before boarding the 15.55 ferry for the short passage to Mull. George, Liz (and their campervan) were already on the island and Lynda followed on a later ferry. Craignure was very handy for those staying in the Craignure Hostel but Tom, Jim, Andrew and I embarked on a 10 mile ride to our accommodation in the Salen Hotel, unsurprisingly in Salen, which is right in the centre of the island.

After a comfortable night we were up early the next day for our island tour.

Day 1: Island Tour

We assembled at Salen for our "pannier bags free" clockwise tour on single track roads with passing places. Lynda and Ned cycled up from the hostel. Liz and George arrived in their campervan, though George was not riding on this trip due to recent knee surgery.

After just 10 undulating miles the seven of us reached the **Ulva ferry** to access this remote community owned island. It has no roads and no vehicular traffic.

We arrived at 10.15 and purchased coffee in the Boat House coffee shop. Yes, a little early but opportunities on Mull are few and far between so you have to grab them when you can. We had a most enjoyable walk exploring the deserted island (once inhabited by 300 kelp farmers). We were pleased to hear that efforts are being made to repopulate the island and rebuild the

181

abandoned crofts. The island is a rare haven of peace.

Back on Mull, we remounted to continue our circuit with 12 hilly and challenging miles between Ulva and Calgary Beach. Earlier in the week, George had driven the circuit in his campervan and was able to warn us of the steep gradients and gruesome hairpin bends ahead, so some bike pushing was inevitable.

Calgary beach

182

At Calgary Beach the sun was shining, the sands were silver, and the sea turquoise, so three of us went for a swim in the Atlantic. Despite being a participant in periodic cold water sea swimming, this was by far the coldest I'd ever swum in!

We lunched at the excellent Calgary Art Centre Cafe before continuing for an even hillier 12 miles to Tobermory. Mr. Noon had not been kidding about the island being "a bit hilly".

Tobermory is the interesting and pretty main town, nay, capital, of Mull – a mixture of marine commerce and tourist attractions. We sampled afternoon tea at the Pier Cafe on Tobermory's harbour front. Andrew and Jim visited the Tobermory Distillery only to find that the day's tours had been cancelled. But, "Oh Joy!" As compensation, they were invited to sample as many whiskies as they wished, free of charge. So they did!

The climb out of Tobermory was a brutal reminder of Mull's hilly terrain but the 10 undulating miles back to Salen was very scenic. As Tom, Andrew, Jim and I tucked into our evening meal we wondered what the table service was like in the bunkhouse.

Day 2: Non cycling options
On day two the bikes remained parked as each of the group undertook a different but active option:

Andrew, Jim, Ned and Lynda climbed Ben More, the only Munro on the island. I ran the Mull Half Marathon to commemorate my 70th birthday, accompanied by Liz. Tom took two pleasant walks in and around Tobermory, whilst George used the campervan to transport the climbers to the foot of the mountain. Whist awaiting their return, he decided to re-park the campervan a little nearer to the loch's edge. Unluckily the rear wheels sank into soft ground and despite emptying all of the weight out, the campervan remained stuck.

But luckily, even with a very poor mobile phone signal, he managed to contact Green Flag who send a recovery vehicle out to him. It was based a few miles down the road. The four up on the mountain could see a multitude of yellow flashing lights below and wondered if ET had landed.

The half marathon was run in persistent drizzle, but runners quite like this. The event was really well organised with water stations every 3 miles, friendly marshalls and mile markers all the way back to Salen. Liz finished 20 seconds ahead of me. I was pleased with my time (2:23) but I was even more delighted to be awarded the "Oldest finisher in the race" prize – a lovely engraved glass shield plus a basket containing local produce – Tobermory whisky, cheese, smoked trout, fudge, biscuits and soap.

After our meal in the Salen Hotel, Tom, Andrew and Jim persuaded me that I couldn't possibly fit my basket of goodies into my pannier bags, so we ate all of the cheese and drank all of the whisky. The whisky was so good we spent the evening ordering a few more tots from the hotel bar. (Tough on those in the hostel!)

Day 3: Cycle to Iona

We assembled outside our hotel at 09.00 for our 39 mile ride from Salen to Fionnphort.

The scenery was stunning – calm lochs, gushing waterfalls and rugged overhanging cliffs. We were on the lookout for Sea Eagles but disappointingly, failed to spot any. But we did spot George and Liz's campervan in a lay-by. They'd generously laid on bacon rolls and coffee. I donated my roll to Ned. We left them to the cleaning up as we continued around the coast and up on to another high point. The descent was long and exhilarating.

Continuing on, we were approaching the Argyle Arms in Bunessan when we felt a few spits and spots of rain but we were due to stop there for lunch anyway.

Coincidentally, "Bunessan" is a hymn tune based on a Scottish folk melody and named after the very same village of Bunessan. It was first associated with the Christmas Carol, "Child in the Manger" and later, (and more commonly), with Cat Stevens' "Morning Has Broken".

After a really good lunch at the Argyle Arms we had just 5 undulating miles to ride to the Iona ferry. Unfortunately, the rain was so heavy we were soon soaked right through. Arriving at Fionnphort, we boarded the ferry. It is just a 10 minute crossing.

Iona is also an oasis of calm with no vehicles. It has a Christian retreat, an Abbey, an ancient burial place for Scottish kings, a ruined nunnery but best of all, the sumptuous St Columba Hotel, where four of us were booked in.

Iona Abbey

I was so wet I was dripping water all over the reception floor. Desperate for a hot bath, I secured a free upgrade to a room with Loch view and, indeed, a large bath! I won't say Tom was seething but he'd arrived before me and was disappointed he hadn't thought of asking for an upgrade too. But even with just a shower, he was better off than Andrew, Jim and Ned who were in a four-bedded "pod" with a walk across a wet field to the toilet block. As I've said elsewhere, I do prefer my home comforts.

That evening, the eight of us had our end-of-tour dinner in the hotel.

Day 4: Sailing and sightseeing

Following breakfast, five of us took a pre-booked boat trip from Iona to the island of Staffa to view Fingal's Cave.

What a great excursion – we saw sea otters, basking seals and dolphins on our voyage out, before landing on Staffa. We opted to view the cave before the rest of the passengers, making our way along a tricky path with cable handrail. Our photographs were all the better for having no other people in view. The cave is spectacular and well worth the visit.

The entrance to Fingal's Cave, Staffa

We then climbed on to the top of the island to watch the puffins coming and going with food for their young before our one hour stay was up. We boarded the boat for a calm crossing back to Iona.

Tom and I decided to delay our lunch so left the others as we caught an early ferry back to Mull and start our 34 mile cycle to Craignure and our ferry to the mainland.

We retraced our rain swept cycle from the previous day. This was a completely different ride along the peninsula looking towards the best of Mull's scenery. But still no Sea Eagles!

Purchasing lunch may have presented a problem had we not encountered a remote Post Office where we received a very warm welcome from the proprietress who provided pots of tea and yummy homemade sandwiches.

While we rested, Ned, Jim and Andrew cycled past before Lynda, Liz and George arrived in the camper van. Their offer to take our pannier bags to the ferry terminal seemed a great idea. After they'd chucked them in the van and left,

I immediately realised that all my bike tools and spare inner tubes were in the bags.

We'd covered 18 miles since leaving Iona so had 16 to do to the ferry terminal but with a considerable climb in between. Blow me, as soon as we set off, the rain started and the mist descended totally obscuring what would have been a stunning view as we rode up the glen and over the pass. The descent into Craignure was equally as exhilarating as the previous day's except it felt like we were riding into a sprinkler hose on the highest setting.

Arriving in Craignure at 5.15, we were just 10 minutes too late for the ferry. Luckily we located our pannier bags leaning against the hostel wall before we sought warmth and shelter in the Calmac office and gift shop. Here we spent a happy half hour poring over the gifts while at the same time pouring drips all over their floor.

We boarded the 18.25 ferry and secured the best seats. As gentlemen, it was only right that we should move along to accommodate a young family. It was soon after that we realised they would now have suspiciously damp bottoms.

At Oban, we disembarked and made our way to our accommodation close by.

Ned was in the Corran House Hostel and later told us that he'd shared a room with a large Italian lady. He added that he had to avert his gaze when she started changing into her PJ's. Jim and Andrew jumped into their car and, after a hearty portion of fish and chips, headed south. Liz and George also hit the road south in their campervan, staying over at Balloch. Lynda met a group of walking friends to continue her holiday.

That just left Tom and me who were in a decent standard of hotel. The tiny single rooms measured about 7' x 10' but more importantly I had a bath with lashings of hot water to wallow in and a window that opened. Tom fared less well. Not only was his room heating on full blast but the window was stuck fast. Fine, if you like sleeping in a Turkish steam room, but poor Tom had little sleep. The next day, he managed to secure a full refund.

Day 5: Home again

Remote island cycling is great but the travel logistics are complicated. Some of our riders will only tour from, and/or to, home. We'd had a great holiday so I did not mind the 3 hour train journey to Glasgow. Tom, Ned and I had a superb lunch next to the River Clyde at the Hilton Garden Inn before joining our trains to Liverpool and Wirral.

9. London to Paris (L2P)

Background

After completing a number of UK tours, it was time to explore further afield. Both commercial and charity versions of **London to Paris** rides are frequently advertised but self planning provides much more satisfaction.

After putting out the word, we eventually ended up with 12 riders aged between 18 and 78 and ranging from experienced to novice. Most were still working so there was a strong lobby to severely limit the number of touring days in order to preserve precious annual leave entitlements. Consequently, the whole tour was condensed to a tight,

and barely do-able, four days –
Saturday to Tuesday.

Day 1: Saturday - Travelling to the start in London

Being of Scottish descent, I begrudged
the outrageous cost of an overnight stay
in a London hotel, preferring an early
morning start from my home on the
Wirral Peninsula.

After a light breakfast I wheeled my
previously prepared bike out of the
porch and I made my way round to
Fred's house where I was relieved to
find he was all ready to leave.

We commenced our ride at 04.30.
Despite it being June, it felt very cold as
we sped downhill towards Birkenhead
centre. Everywhere was deserted
except, of course, for the area around

the nightclubs. Here, we encountered loud "drum 'n' bass" music and despite it being broad daylight, crowds of lightly clad men and women were stumbling out of the clubs. "Don't make eye contact," I suggested to Fred as we felt more than a little ridiculous cycling through the drunken masses in our Lycra shorts.

Next was the Mersey Tunnel (open to cycles until 6am). Despite fairly light traffic, the booming noise of taxis roaring up behind us was loud and a little scary.

We arrived at Liverpool Lime Street Station where it was easy to load our bikes into our train's on-board bike bay. We departed on time at 05.47. So far, so good.

During our journey we participated in second breakfasts from the buffet car and at 07.55 we pulled in to Euston Station. We were soon riding along a "Cycle London" route through narrow streets and quiet alleyways towards the team's rendezvous point at Big Ben.

On the way, we'd planned to ride down The Mall to say a quick "Good morning" to the Queen at Buckingham Palace. But today was the Trooping of the Colour and we were barred from proceeding. Special Branch must have thought we looked like suspicious pensioner terrorists.

A pleasant detour took in The Cenotaph, Horse Guards Parade and Downing Street, arriving at Big Ben for at 0840. The others appeared from various directions – most had sensibly stayed overnight.

At 0900 all were present and after a couple of photographs, we commenced our journey proper at 09.20:

Ready for the off

London to Newhaven

To plan our route out of London, I had obtained some free "Cycle London" maps which identified a Blue Route (dedicated cycle lane) out of the capital to Sutton Station. Additionally, I had contacted the West Sussex CTC (Cyclists' Touring Club, now called Cycling UK) who had helpfully commented on my route and had suggested a decent coffee stop.

After crossing Westminster Bridge, we sang appropriate songs as we rode along Lambeth Walk ("Oi!") and later, around Amen Corner ("Bend me, shake me", as I recall). Progress was a little slow due to the plethora of traffic signals but eventually the route opened out as we entered Surrey. After several climbs, we reached the eccentric **Fanny's Farm Garden Centre** where we stopped for excellent coffee and scones served by Fanny herself (sadly, neither the farm shop, nor Fanny, is still around).

Suitably refreshed, we proceeded into Sussex (even more climbing) arriving at our lunch stop at Turner's Hill. Although the pub had finished serving meals, the local convenience store had a good selection of sandwiches and drinks for our picnic on the green.

Thereafter the route was both undulating and pretty. We had afternoon tea in Ditchling before heading southeast towards Lewes. This final 15 miles was very fast with some good descents and a following wind. We arrived at the Premier Inn*, Newhaven at 18.00. Checking in was a breeze so I was quickly in the bath.

*Premier Inns are our preferred overnight tour stops – you know what to expect; there's usually a bath available: you can take your bike into your room; and inexpensive meals are available on site.

My evening meal was a delicious vegetable curry plus much rehydration. I slept very well (10 out of 10).

Miles cycled from Wirral to Liverpool (12) and Big Ben to Newhaven (64)

Total miles for the day – 76

Day 2: Sunday - Newhaven to Forges-les-Eaux

After an excellent cooked-to-order full English breakfast we were about to leave the hotel at 08.00 but discovered that one of the party had a flat tyre.

Even with a speedy Formula 1 pit lane tyre change, we could not avoid arriving late at the ferry terminal but, with a Gallic shrug, the crew waved us to the front of the queue. It was so easy to board and store the bikes before going up the stairs to bag the best seats in the lounge.

We had a very smooth crossing. Coffee, Sunday newspapers and lunch on board – bliss! At 14.30, (French time), we docked in Dieppe.

As cyclists, we were allowed off first.

Arrival at Dieppe

It felt warmer than Blighty as we sped off along very quiet roads. After 5 miles we turned on to "The Avenue Verte" – a disused railway line converted into a tarmac surfaced bike route. We stayed on this beautiful route for 25 miles.

The Avenue Verte

Whist traffic-free cycling is good, this route is very straight. In fact, it is so straight that young James fell asleep as he was riding along. He received a rude awakening after drifting off the tarmac on to the grassy verge. Shortly, and seeking a refreshment stop, we pulled in to a caravan park for a cup of tea.

The French are not known for brewing good cups of tea but mine was made undrinkable after James convinced me that a small carton of cream was milk. Tea a la crème – yuk!

We arrived at Le Sof Hotel, Forges-les-Eaux at 18.00. It was very 'Allo, 'Allo. My room was comfortable but far from soundproof! The couple in the next room were clearly enjoying their bath together. Bikes were stored safely in a garage in the yard.

After indulging in a deep, hot and sudsy, wallow myself, I made my way to the bijou restaurant for dinner. Eight of us were staying here. The other four were in a converted barn further down the road.

Our four course set meal was very traditional - crudities and snails, beef bourguignon, cheeseboard, and an ice cream/cake concoction. Two of us were non-meat eaters so Monsieur le Chef concocted a superb cheese and mushroom omelette. All of this washed down with lots of Belgian beer and red wine. Some of the lads imbibed in cognac to finish but there was a long ride ahead the next day.

I retired to bed for 22.30.

Miles cycled Dieppe to Forges: 36
Rolling mileage: – 112

Day 3: Monday - Forges-les-Eaux to Carriere-sous-Poissy

We were all up in time for an 8 o'clock traditional French breakfast before visiting the supermarket to purchase lunch provisions. We were away proper by 0930.

The countryside was stunningly simple with long sweeping fields across very open countryside. The route was undulating with occasional climbs – reminiscent of Dorset.

We had earmarked a bar for our coffee stop in St Germer-de-Fly. It is a beautiful town with stunning cathedral. It was just a pity that much of France is closed on a Monday.

St Germer-de-Fly cathedral

I used my schoolboy French to ask a passer-by where I might obtain "une tasse de cafe". Her reply was rapid and largely unintelligible but she seemed to be directing us to an out of town supermarket accessed via a four lane by-pass. Luckily, a friendly businessman spotted our dilemma and opened up some sort of youth club, serving mugs of latte at one euro apiece as we sat at tables made from painted oil drums.

We pressed on until lunch at St Crepin where we ate our sandwiches in the lovely village square. More undulating miles followed before we reached Carriere-sous-Poissy and the Auberge Des Ecluses Hotel by the banks of the Seine and within sight of a distant Eiffel Tower.

As we approached the hotel, I rode over a speed bump, dislodging a pannier bag which in turn hit my rear mudguard causing it to fold under itself. The use of some brute force straightened it sufficiently to complete the trip.

The Auberge Des Ecluses Hotel is small with just eight bedrooms. It was reminiscent of The Addams Family's house with a large and creaking wooden staircase and ancient furnishings everywhere.

After the day's ride, we were so thirsty we walked a short distance to a local bar for a pre-shower beer or three.

My bedroom interior

Back at the hotel, we all met up for dinner. The a la carte menu was impressive with octopus as one of the choices. We had some difficulty deciphering what else was on offer – we had just a smattering of schoolboy French between us and the waiter spoke no English. I had a crab salad starter, a perch (I think) for my main course and an ice cream dessert.

Throughout the meal the waiter kept bringing out more and more bottles of wine, gesticulating an assurance that this was all included in the price.

I staggered to bed for 22.30 (sleep rating 10 out of 10)

Miles cycled: Forges to Carriere sous Poissy – 64
Rolling mileage – 176

Day 4: Tuesday - Carriers-sous-Poissy to Paris

The schedule for today was going to be tight if we were to complete the 25 miles into Paris, have some lunch, ride nine miles on my tour of the city and then a further 22 miles to the airport in time to board our flight.

We'd ordered an eight o'clock breakfast. This was excellent with lashings of fruit salad, an absolutely massive cheeseboard plus as many croissants as we could possibly eat. Oh, and unlimited coffee, too.

Unfortunately, our scheduled 0900 start was delayed due to an unseemly dispute over the bill. We believed that we had booked half board with dinner included but the scary manager seemed to be saying that the previous evening's a la carte meal was not included in the room rate. We really needed to get on the road so after some pathetic negotiating using our equally pathetic schoolboy French, we agreed a stupidly hefty price before departing at 0920.

The route was very busy over the Seine bridge and through the town of Poissy but after just two miles we entered the first of the seven glorious traffic-free forest cycle paths that would lead us to all the way to Paris. Pre-Garmin, this was the hardest part to navigate but we only needed a couple of pauses to consult the map. We made reasonable progress until a heavy rain shower persuaded us to stop at a forest café for coffee. This turned into snacks and, with little sign of the rain going off, a longer stop. I found myself looking at my watch.

In no rush to saddle up!

Finally rolling again, this royal parks route was a delight - almost completely traffic free. We eventually emerged in St Cloud. I'd heard that St Cloud has some connection with Edith Piaf but we did not have time to stop - I had no regrets. We crossed The Seine by a footbridge into the Bois Boulogne for a cycle path all the way to the Eiffel Tower. We arrived later than I'd hoped for, at 14.00.

After pausing for the usual, "This is us in front of the Eiffel Tower" photographs, we commenced "Ian's bike tour of

Paris". Jim pulled me to one side, concernedly asking, "Ian, are you sure we've got time for this?" (Secretly, I thought we didn't but I'd never been to Paris before and I did not wish to waste the short talks I'd carefully prepared for each historic site). "Yes", I fibbed.

My tour took in Napoleon's tomb, L'hopital des Invalides and the Place de la Concorde before we rode up the busy Champs Elysee to the Arc de Triomph. At this point, we were clearly behind schedule so I threw my history talks into a waste bin.

Napoleon's tomb

Riding back down the Champs Elysee, we weaved in and out of four lanes of teatime traffic with Adam shouting "Bon jour" at the drivers of standing cars. It was an exciting ride back to the Place de la Concorde. Soon we were at the Louvre Gallery and after a brief stop, Notre Dame Cathedral.

The Louvre

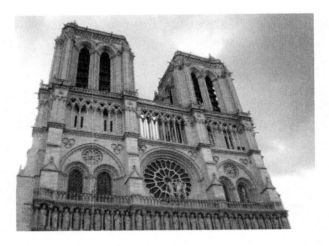

Notre Dame Cathedral

The advantage of city touring on a bike is that you can cycle in and out of narrow alleyways and right up to the sights.

We arrived at the Bastille Square at 16.40 and though we needed to press on, I had to agree to a short loo break.

Paris to Charles de Gaulle airport

The ride out of Paris took us along the wide, well-surfaced towpath of the Canal St Martin. We were making satisfactory progress until we came to part which was closed for repair. The detour took us into a housing estate. A bit disorientated, I took out my map and asked a one word question to a passer-by, "Airport?".

Other cyclists will have experienced the usual response where a non-cyclist thinks like a car driver and this occasion proved to be no exception. We refused to take his advice to cycle down the main dual carriageway and after a bit of lateral thinking we found our own way back to our route on the canal towpath. Eventually minor roads took us to the perimeter of the airport and we arrived in the passenger concourse just before our check-in closed, at 19.30. Phew!

Packing the bikes was well rehearsed with pedals removed and handlebars turned. The bikes were slid into plastic CTC cycle bags and taped. The airport staff opened a special check-in desk for us and there was no problem accepting the bikes, apart from the guy insisting that all tyres must be deflated. So, after fumbling around to locate the tyre valves, at last the bikes were checked in and we went airside to grab a cold beer to replace lost fluids.

After a short flight we arrived in Liverpool for 22.15.

We recovered our bikes from the carousel and after assembly and tyre inflation. (Thanks to Jill for meeting us with a track pump) the five of us who were not being picked up set off along deserted streets towards the city centre. We arrived at the Liver Building at 23.50.

The Mersey Tunnel was extremely quiet. We had a good ride through and there was no hassle from other vehicles. After saying our farewells Fred, Adam, and I rode off through an equally quiet Birkenhead. I arrived home, sweaty and starving, at half past midnight.

Miles cycled:
Carriere-sous-Poissy to Eiffel Tower: 25
Tour of Paris: 9
Bastille to home: 41
Day total: 75

Total tour miles: 251

The next day I had a lie in before taking my time unpacking, cleaning my bike and regaling my wife, Chris, with tales of my adventure. Jim did not have it quite so easy. On the plane, he'd told me he was due to make a presentation on leadership to a group of trainees at 08.30.

10. Land's End to John O'Groats

Background

I have always liked marking my big birthdays - 30th (a Farewell to 20's party); 40th (a "Black and White" fancy dress party) and 50th (running the London Marathon).

For my 60th birthday, I chose that classic British ride – Land's End to John O'Groats, (also known as "LeJog", the "End to End" or "E2E").

After a bit of research, I discounted solo riding in favour of an organised tour. The advantages were; pre-booked accommodation, luggage taken on ahead, a qualified bike mechanic riding with the group and at the end of the trip, my bike delivered to my front door.

I accepted the last remaining place on the "Bike Adventures" tour commencing on 14th July 2007. Unfortunately, 2007 was the year of the worst flooding in England since the Middle Ages – the year when Tewkesbury was completely cut off.

Not only did I choose the wrong year, but I also made some silly schoolboy errors over my chosen bike. I thought my Claude Butler hybrid bike would be fine but it turned out to be far too heavy and slow.

The second problem was the tyres. In the pre-tour blurb we were advised to fit new tyres, preferably "Continentals". Naively, I had no idea that Continentals were actually a brand of puncture-resistant tyres. Instead, I went to Halfords, asked what new tyres they had in stock and paid the bargain price of £7.00 each. Big mistake!

Problem three was my lack of training. These days I can knock off my weekly 60 or 70 mile ride with ease, but pre-End to End, I had done little training other than one 40 mile ride round a very flat Cheshire loop a couple of weeks before the trip.

Lastly, I had no idea about clothing. I had no cleats, nor toe clips. My training shoes were not knobbly enough to grip the pedals, so when it rained, my shoes kept slipping forwards. Also, my selection of short sleeved tee shirts proved to be too thin to retain body temperature.

But hey, I thought I was good to go.

Pre-ride: Travelling to Land's End and the tour start

At 10.00 my bike, travelling bag and I were dropped off at Chester Station for a very tedious train ride to Penzance. After three different trains, and a stiff bottom, I arrived at Penzance at 6.30 pm.

I'd half an hour to kill before being met by the van so I'd arranged to go for a cup of tea with my mate, Dave, who'd recently relocated to Penzance. He didn't appear. He told me later he was having a carpet laid and he'd completely forgotten. Instead, I had the pleasure of chatting to Vikki who was riding in the same group to John O'Groats. Vikki was celebrating her 40th birthday.

The van arrived and we were whisked off to The Land's End Hotel where we parked our bikes in the ballroom. Oh dear! What a shock – thirteen road bikes plus a mountain bike and mine!

At the dinner table I met my fellow travellers. Someone asked, "Have you seen that tank in the ballroom. I wonder who'll be riding that monster."

Day One (Sat 14th July):
Land's End to Bodmin (70.1 miles)

After receiving our tour shirts and turn-by-turn route instructions, we assembled for a team photograph. At 09.30 we started our adventure.

I was immediately dropped by the group and for much of the day I cycled alone.

The route went along the north coast of Cornwall through Perranporth. I remember stopping for coffee at Hale when it was really lunchtime. Here the guy on the mountain bike caught me up. My log reads, "Blue skies and a following breeze" but there were many very steep hills. I finally rolled into Bodmin well past 7pm.

The guy on the mountain bike fared worse. Twenty miles short of Bodmin his pedals seized up and he had to be rescued by the broom wagon.

Day Two (Sun 15th July): Bodmin to Whiddon Down (near Exeter) (54.9 miles)

Though this day's mileage seems comparatively low, it was more than compensated for by some long and arduous climbing firstly over Bodmin

Moor and then Dartmoor where, for long periods, I was riding in dense low cloud.

The ponies looked cute, though, and the 1780 historic Clapper Bridge over the River Dart was worthy of a misty photo stop:

At our evening meal, I discovered that one of our front riders, Don, had crashed badly whilst descending a waterlogged and gravel-covered descent and was in hospital.

Day Three (Monday 16th July): Whiddon Down (Near Exeter) to Bawdrip (near Bridgewater) (64 miles)

The sun cream and sunglasses came out for another challenging day of hill climbing, this time through the northern hills of Devon and into Somerset.

During late afternoon, there was one particularly long and hard climb over the Quantock Hills. Once at the top, I took a breather as I caught my first glimpse of the Bristol Channel. As I was catching my breath, a farmer came over to chat. He told me he was still ploughing and combining at 78 (he looked about 55). Once he'd discovered I was riding End to End, he recounted a story about a party of nudist End to Enders who'd asked to sleep in his barn. "They were all totally starkers - even the women!" he exclaimed, seemingly not believing that nudist hikers are actually unclothed.

The descent into Bridgewater was the best part of the day.

Day Four (Tuesday 17th July): Bawdrip (near Bridgewater) to Monmouth (78 miles)

My day started with a superb farmhouse breakfast overlooking the dairy herd being brought in for milking, (and one cow being lifted out of ditch with a couple of wide straps attached to a fork-lift truck – not sure the Health and Safety Executive would approve).

It turned out to be a very long day with 12 hours in the saddle. The persistent rain didn't help and prevented me from fully appreciating the otherwise gorgeous Cheddar Gorge.

A sequence of waterlogged lanes, with much mud and debris, dulled my spirits. My front tyre punctured and after changing the tube, it immediately deflated again. It wasn't until the third occasion that I found a minute piece of flint in the tyre.

Eventually, I arrived in the outskirts of Bristol.

Crossing the suspension bridge into South Wales was spectacular and, when you're on a bike, you can stop halfway across to admire the views. The Wye Valley from Chepstow to Monmouth provided an opportunity for better progress. Tintern Abbey was serene in the late evening sunshine. I finally arrived in Monmouth at 8pm.

We heard that Don was out of hospital but would be riding in the van for the next few days to aid recuperation.

Day 5 (Wednesday 18th July): Monmouth to Wentnor (near Shrewsbury) (72.6 miles)

Today was a beautiful summer's day with a light wind. But before starting I needed to borrow a bucket of water and cloth to clean all the previous day's grime from my bike and chain. Some of the group were so grumpy about the effects of yesterday's mucky route on their road bikes that they abandoned the official instructions and rode A roads instead!

I stuck with the official itinerary and after an hour's worth of beautiful hill riding, out of Monmouth, we progressed through undulating and pretty Hereford and Shropshire.

The only incident of note was when a mature and rather plump lady on a horse did not look to her left as she emerged from a field. The horse was startled by my sudden and silent approach and bolted. After much frothing and bucking, the rider finally managed to regain control but it was her own fault - she should have looked first.

Despite the 72 mile distance, I made good time today.

Day Six (Thursday 19th July): Wentnor (near Shrewsbury) to Little Leigh (near Northwich) (72.2 miles)

A sunny day, with no wind meant some faster riding today. I was back on my home territory and well on target for the lunch stop in Malpas when my front tyre developed a hernia, or, as they say in the trade, it "egged". Almost immediately, it blew, leaving a large hole in my £7.00 tyre.

With no means of repairing such a large gash, I lost two hours waiting for the mechanic who carried some spare tyres on the van. My overnight stop was the nearest point on the trip to my home so I'd arranged for my family to join me for dinner. I had to do some hard riding to make up the lost time.

Just two miles from my B&B, my rear tyre also developed an egg but luckily didn't blow. (These days, our weekly cycling group often rides along this stretch of road where I am always reminded of the egged tyres).

The evening meal was excellent and I was cheered up by seeing my family.

Day Seven (Friday 20th July): Little Leigh to Clitheroe (65.2 Miles)

Oh, how I appreciated flat Cheshire as we headed north to cross the River Mersey and Manchester Ship Canal.

After urban Warrington and Leigh, we continued via the picturesque Rivington

240

Reservoir and over Winter Hill into a strong headwind. You know it's a strong headwind when you have to pedal going down the descents.

The hills around Bolton and Blackburn were very challenging and a little unwelcome, especially at the end of the day, but I arrived at my destination by 5pm. This was a first.

In Clitheroe, two of us were staying in a pub. Gray and I ate out with the rest of the group but on our return to the pub, we spied a van parked outside and observed roadies carrying large speakers inside. "Disco night, tonight", said the barman as we collected our keys.

When I am on these tours, I like a really early night so was in bed by 9.30pm.

Soon afterwards, some very loud "doof, doof, doof" music started, right beneath my bedroom. "Crikey", I thought, "I'll never sleep through that lot". I remember hearing the start of the second track before drifting off into a deep slumber.

The next morning Gray and I went down for breakfast but found we were alone inside a locked pub. Breakfast was not served until 08.30, the time the staff arrived. Goodness knows what would have happened if there had been a fire.

Day Eight (Saturday 21st July): Clitheroe to Kirkby Stephen (56.7 Miles)

Gray and I set off together climbing up to Slaidburn. Here, he carried straight on in the direction of Dent Village but I went "off piste" to take in Settle and the

Ribblesdale Valley. It was a trip down memory lane for me as I had completed the Three Peaks of Yorkshire Challenge a few years earlier.

My brief stop at the Horton in Ribblesdale Visitor Centre marked the halfway point of the End to End.

Later, whilst enjoying a mug of tea at a rainy Ribblehead Viaduct tea van, a guy commented on my bike – "Bet that's reliable", he said. That's as maybe, I thought, but it was hard work.

I rejoined the official route at Cowgill before embarking on the long, steep and daunting ascent passing Britain's highest railway station. It is called Dent Station even though it is 4 miles from Dent village. Unfortunately, soon after I'd starting grinding up this single track road, a single decker bus came up behind me. I had two choices - to continue pedalling for 20 or 30 minutes at 3mph with a bus up my backside, or to pull over and risk not getting started again. I pulled over. The driver was most appreciative but I wasn't. Attempting my restart on a 25% hill was difficult. I had to ride across the narrow lane and hope to gain sufficient momentum to keep going.

Once over Garsdale Summit, the route was much easier and I arrived at my B&B in Kirkby Stephen at 5.30.

Great scenery today but the weather was challenging - heavy rain most of the day and strong headwinds

Day Nine (Sunday 22nd July): Kirkby Stephen to Ecclefechan (72.2 Miles)

After a good night's sleep in a top class B&B I was off again by 08.30 aided by a good tail wind. The Lakeland hills to my left looked spectacular. Each day, my lunch menu was a portion of that cycling stalwart - beans on toast, though the price varied every time – anything between £2.50 and £6.50.

In the afternoon, another watershed moment - we crossed the border into Scotland, near to Longtown.

I'd earlier arranged to meet my Scottish cousin and his wife for an evening meal at our hotel in Ecclefechan but I'd underestimated my arrival time. Consequently I had to "put the hammer down" to make the rendezvous.

It was a good meal and great to catch up with my Scottish relatives.

Day Ten (Monday 23rd July): Ecclefechan to Motherwell (70 Miles)

Today, Don left the van and gingerly rejoined the ride. He was very battered and bruised with large scabs on his head and face.

The route took us on the old A74 – now a dedicated cycle route, through Lockerbie, Crawford and Abington. At Lesmahagow we commenced a ten-mile grind through the outskirts of Glasgow but I now know where the football team, Hamilton Academicals, play.

Approaching Motherwell, the heavy traffic was scary but we were soon in the beautiful and peaceful Strathclyde Park and our overnight stay at a Toby Grill.

Strathclyde Country Park

Day Eleven (Tuesday 24th July): Motherwell to Inveraray (82 Miles)

The day started with a warning from our ride leader that due to the risk of muggings on the Clyde cycle path through Glasgow, we'd be having a delayed start (at 09.00) and for safety in numbers, we'd be riding as one group. This was no use to me as with 82 miles to cover, I needed my 08.00 start, so I rode off with the ride leader's "On your own head be it, Ian" ringing in my ears.

After leaving Motherwell I soon picked up the riverside path. Initially it went through some dodgy areas of deprivation. There was graffiti everywhere and many patches of broken glass. A couple of scruffy men on a bench were enjoying a liquid breakfast from a bottle inside a brown paper bag.

At one particularly remote spot, I was stopped by two toughs coming the other way on bikes.

"Oh, heck" I thought, "Here we go. I should have listened".

"Aw wight, Mite", said the first in Estuary English, "Is dis the wight weigh for "Lock" Lomond?"

"Err, no" I replied, "totally the wrong way"

"Aw, wight. See, the fing is, we're doin' Leand's End to John a'Gwoats"

"So am I", I said.

"Gweat!" Can we wide wiv you?"

They introduced themselves as Pete and Phil, two prison officers from Essex. I told them about the dire warnings in my early morning briefing and they told me not to worry as they undertook to ensure my safe passage.

The cycleway alongside the River Clyde

So we travelled the next 20 miles as a trio. I learned a lot about life in prison and the difficult cases that prison officers have to deal with. During beans on toast at a cafe just shy of Balloch, I told them about my old mum who lived in an assisted flat. They were amused when I told them that the flats warden was previously a prison officer. They visualised him shoving the elderly residents through their front doors and shouting, "Get back in yer cell!"

Loch Lomond

At Loch Lomond the two lads took a different route as I continued over the Fruin Pass to Arrochar. Later, I crawled up the seemingly never ending four mile

Rest-and-be-Thankful Pass to meet some of my E2E group at the top.

Rest and be Thankful (I did, and I was)

The scenery was superb. Descending again was exhilarating. It was a bit too fast for me though. I started braking when I hit 37mph but others made 50.

Our evening stop was in Inverary on the banks of Loch Fyne so it was only right to have a Scottish fish supper for my evening meal.

Day Twelve (Wednesday 25th July): Inverary to Fort William (74 Miles)

A slow and inefficient breakfast service, plus a broken gear cable as soon as I set off, meant a 10.30am start from the back of the grid.

However, once underway, I overdosed on the fantastic scenery as we moved from the Trossachs to the Highlands. The weather today was amazingly good, with brief showers giving way to lovely sunshine and a helpful following wind.

At Fort William, I joined the others for an Indian meal where I was dismayed to hear that Don was back in hospital with septicaemia.

Day Thirteen (Thursday 26th July):
Fort William to Evanton (North of Inverness) (80 Miles)

It was a "monster day" today!

That's monster miles - 80; monster rain - but just for final 4 miles; and a monster in a loch - Loch Ness.

At Spean Bridge and the start of the Great Glen, we were given the choice of continuing on the A82, or taking a quieter route on the western side of the glen but involving long stretches of forest trail. I chose the latter but once committed I regretted my decision. It was too late to turn back. The trail surface started well but became gloopy in places and it was difficult to ride any quicker than 8mph.

Eventually, I rejoined the A82 at a point where there was a further choice for the next part of the ride into Fort Augustus - to either ride alongside the Caledonian Canal, or remain on the A82. After the previous difficult miles, I chose to stay on the road. This also turned out to be the wrong choice. When I met the others at the lunch stop, those who'd cycled along the canal told me the surface was excellent and the scenery spectacular.

After lunch, one of the guys was describing how he'd slightly buckled his rear wheel but it was OK to ride. Famous last words! He mounted up, his wheel disintegrated and he ended up sitting in the road on top of a pile of spokes.

The views of Loch Ness were stunning as we reached Urquart Castle but Nessie was having a day off. Anyway, there was no time for monster spotting as we turned away from the Great Glen to conquer the feared Drumnadrochit Pass (1mile of 1 in 6) towards Dingwall. People had been dreading this climb for a few days but it was do-able in a very low gear.

Just as we were approaching Evanton, there was really heavy (Hollywood style) rain. Had I jumped into Loch Ness, I wouldn't have been any wetter.

That evening, over dinner, I heard that Vikki had quit the ride after a massive falling out with her room-mate. She was planning to ride on solo and be met at John O'Groats by her husband who was already on his way to collect her. A disappointing end to what should have been a memorable trip, but my rule is never to share a room, especially with a stranger.

Day Fourteen 14 (Friday 27th July):
Evanton to Bettyhill (77 miles)

This morning I was comforted to hear that one of the other riders had overtaken my record of punctures so I didn't feel so bad about my earlier problems.

I had another early start and a picturesque climb to view the Dornoch Estuary before whizzing downhill to Dornoch itself. Later, I joined the group for great coffee and chocolate cake at the Falls of Shin Visitor Centre.

We then entered the remote county of Sutherland and picked up an annoying wind plus horizontal rain for the next 17 miles of open moorland. The isolated Crask Inn provided some very welcome respite, with a log fire and hot soup.

After lunch, the rain diminished, the route veered north east and the wind seemed to be on our backs. On one lonely stretch I shall never forget the moment when a red deer ran alongside me for a while before crossing the road just ahead of my front wheel. At Bettyhill, I reached the top of Scotland, and the sea – what a stunningly beautiful beach with nobody on it.

The beach at Bettyhill

The Bettyhill Hotel was a curious establishment set in a 1950's time warp but the group evening meal was good.

Day Fifteen (Saturday 28th July): Bettyhill to John O'Groats (51 miles)

Shame that the weather for our final day's riding across the top of Scotland consisted of blustery wind, Scotch mist and showers. Also, the road is very undulating with steep drops into bays and steep climbs back out of them. I'd love to say that the scenery was anything other than the reality - bleak, featureless and treeless.

We past a forlorn and closed Doun Reay power station:

We pushed on to Thurso for a welcome lunch stop in our first busy town for many days. From here, three of us cycled together counting down the miles to John O'Groats but not before just one more tea and scones stop, five miles from the finish.

We crossed the misty and rainy finishing line in formation before the customary photographs and a glass of bubbly.

Before dinner all bikes were loaded into the van.

Day Sixteen (Sunday 29th July): Travelling home again

Today was my wedding anniversary. (Aren't wives good about allowing husbands to indulge in their hobbies?)

After breakfast we boarded a mini-coach and were driven to Inverness Station where the majority caught trains home.

Four of us were taken to the airport where I'd booked a flight to Manchester. My wife collected me and we were home for 5.30. To my amazement, the van arrived with my bike at 7.30, and the crew still had about 220 miles to drive back to their depot in Slough.

Summary:

My total distance was 1040 miles at an average speed of 9.2 mph. I rode for 15 consecutive days starting at around 8.30 and finishing at around 5.30.

My three punctures on day four were really the same puncture three times – I just couldn't see the tiny fragment of flint stuck in my tyre. Across the whole group, we experienced 16 punctures, three snapped gear cables, one slightly buckled wheel, one seized pedal, one total wheel collapse and one bottom bracket problem. A trip like this certainly tests the machine. I had no trouble with midges in Scotland.

The best parts of the trip were the Yorkshire Dales, the Scottish Highlands, the red deer running alongside me, the characters I met on the way and the fact that when you are on a bike, you can easily stop to admire a view or take a photograph.

Appendix - "Kit list"

After organising many cycling tours, I have come up with a checklist of kit recommendations. It is constantly being added to and updated. This is what it looked like for my last tour. Items to take will vary depending upon the length of the tour and remoteness from bike shops

Mobile phone numbers:
Cyclists in the group:
Transport providers:
Hotels:

Essentials:
Train tickets
Ferry tickets
Hotel/B&B booking details
Credit card(s)
Cash
Route instructions
Luggage/Pannier bags
Navigation aids – Garmin and maps

Bike clothes:
Cycling shorts and/or longs
Cycle shirts
Cycle helmet
Skull cap for winter touring
Cycling socks – waterproof if possible
Cycling gloves – winter and/or summer
Goggles/glasses
Waterproof jacket
Shoes to cycle in
Bum bag for cash, tissues, tickets, banana, mini Mars bars, mobile phone etc

Evening clothes:
Jumper or sweatshirt
Lightweight shoes
Lightweight trousers

Other kit:
Mobile phone
Alarm clock (if mobile
phone has no built-in
alarm)
Camera
Small bag with
toothbrush,
toothpaste, shaving
gel, razor
Bin liner to keep clean
clothes dry
Bin liner for laundry
List of Mobile
numbers
Phone charger
Sun cream
Loo paper
Small First Aid kit
Small towel

Bike kit:
Bike computer set to
miles

Drink bottle
Pump and correct
adapter
Lock
Map holder

**Some Tools and
spares you may
consider taking
(could be shared):**

Best to take:
Spare tube(s)
Puncture repair kit –
patches, glue, levers,
chalk, tweezers
Allen Keys

Might like to take:
Pliers
Screwdrivers (flat and
cross)
Disposable rubber
gloves
Cable ties
Spare brake and gear
cables
Chain splitter
Spoke adjuster
Bungee straps

About the author

Ian Cameron is a retired NHS Manager who, from his mid twenties, has attempted to lead a healthy lifestyle through circuit training classes, running and eating a non-meat diet.

He took up cycling in his mid 40's, initially on a series of cheap and inappropriate bikes. He currently rides a Hewitt Touring bike and a Specialized Tarmac road bike. He organises a weekly cycling group in Wirral and is a member of the local council's Active Travel Forum. Cycle touring forms a major part of his annual holiday plans.

As regards writing, in his previous corporate life, Ian edited company newsletters and drafted chairmen's speeches. More recently he has contributed articles to cycling publications. Currently, his light hearted weekly ride reports have prompted members of his cycling group to frequently comment, "Ian, you should write a book".

Contact the author via his agent: iechalmers@btinternet.com

266

Printed in Great Britain
by Amazon